master class
kung fu

D1202647

796.815 G622
Goodman, Fay.
Masterclass Kung fu
                    15.95

MID-CONTINENT PUBLIC LIBRARY
Blue Springs North Branch
850 N.W. Hunter Drive   **BN**
Blue Springs, Mo. 64015

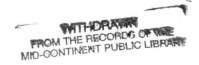
WITHDRAWN
FROM THE RECORDS OF THE
MID-CONTINENT PUBLIC LIBRARY

master class
kungfu

fay goodman

tae kwondo · tai chi · kendo · iaido · shinto ryu

southwater

MID-CONTINENT PUBLIC LIBRARY

3 0000 12294325 5

MID-CONTINENT PUBLIC LIBRARY
Blue Springs North Branch
850 N.W. Hunter Drive
Blue Springs, Mo. 64015

BN

This edition is published by Southwater

Distributed in the UK by
The Manning Partnership
251–253 London Road East
Batheaston
Bath BA1 7RL
tel. 01225 852 727
fax 01225 852 852

Distributed in Canada by
General Publishing
895 Don Mills Road
400–402 Park Centre
Toronto, Ontario M3C 1W3
tel. 416 445 3333
fax 416 445 5991

Published in the USA by
Anness Publishing Inc.
27 West 20th Street
Suite 504
New York
NY 10011
fax 212 807 6813

Distributed in Australia by
Sandstone Publishing
Unit 1, 360 Norton Street
Leichhardt
New South Wales 2040
tel. 02 9560 7888
fax 02 9560 7488

All rights reserved. No part of this publication may be reproduced, stored in a retrieval system, or transmitted in any way or by any means, electronic, mechanical, photocopying, recording or otherwise, without the prior written permission of the copyright holder.

Southwater is an imprint of Anness Publishing Limited
Hermes House, 88–89 Blackfriars Road, London SE1 8HA
tel. 020 7401 2077; fax 020 7633 9499

© Anness Publishing Limited 1998, 2002

Publisher: JOANNA LORENZ
Project Editors: ALISON MACFARLANE, HELEN WILSON and ZOE ANTONIOU
Designer: LISA TAI
Photographer: MIKE JAMES
Proofreaders: KATE HENDERSON and PENELOPE GOODARE
Production Controller: JOANNA KING

Previously published as part of a larger compendium, *The Ultimate Book of Martial Arts*

10 9 8 7 6 5 4 3 2 1

PICTURE CREDITS
Additional pictures supplied by: **Hulton Getty:** p6, p212. **Tony Stone:** p7 top, p8 top, p9 both, p179, p195 both. **Simon Lailey:** p7 bottom, p8 bottom, p13, p146, p147 both, pp148–9, p162, p163 both, p164, p178 top, p210, p229 both. *Tai Chi International:* p194, p196 top. **Fay Goodman:** p226–8. **Werner Forman Archive:** p211.

THANK YOU

To those who have been kind – thank you
To those who have believed – I am grateful
To those who are sincere – you are deep in my thoughts
So let us never despair
When all appears against us
And the evil ones try to take our heart and soul
For those of you who have believed and never faltered
This is what living is made worthwhile for – I thank you

Fay Goodman

CONTENTS

INTRODUCTION 6

KUNG FU 8
WING CHUN 10
History and philosophy 10
Clothing and equipment 14
Etiquette 15
Exercises 16
Techniques 18
MOK-GAR 26
History and philosophy 26
Clothing and equipment 30
Etiquette 31
Exercises 32
Techniques 34
KICK BOXING 40
History and philosophy 40
Clothing and equipment 44
Etiquette 45
Exercises 46
Techniques 48

TAE KWONDO 54
History and philosophy 56
Clothing and equipment 58
Etiquette 59
Exercises 60
Techniques 62

TAI CHI CHUAN 68
History and philosophy 70
Clothing and equipment 74
Etiquette 75
Exercises 76
Techniques 78

KENDO 84
History and philosophy 86
Clothing and equipment 90
Etiquette 92
Exercises 93
Preparation 94
Techniques 96

IAIDO 100
History and philosophy 102
Clothing and equipment 106
Etiquette 108
Exercises 110
Techniques 111

SHINTO RYU 116
History and philosophy 118
Exercises 120
Techniques 121

Index 128
Acknowledgements 128

INTRODUCTION

There are millions of martial arts practitioners all over the world. Through the disciplines these arts impose, men, women and children of all ages and abilities are actively involved in learning how to improve their awareness, health, fitness, confidence and their capacity to protect themselves.

Inherent in their teaching are the guiding principles of respect, courtesy and self-discipline. The martial arts encourage us to fight the enemy within in an effort to become better people. Combine this attitude with the inner strength one gains from their training, and the rewards are peace of mind and a richer quality of life. While some arts may, superficially, appear to be aggressive, especially when weapons are used, this is far from their true meaning. The use of the sword, for example, in its philosophy and teachings, is concerned with developing the mind and body to work harmoniously together, creating the confidence and ability to avoid confrontation. In the words of Musashi Miyamoto, one of Japan's most famous swordsmen (1584-1645): "We need to win the battle before we enter and in many ways we should never need to draw our sword."

The aim of this book is to give you an insight into a selection of martial arts commonly practised throughout the world today. Within the chapters you will find a brief overview of each martial art's history and philosophy and the essential clothing and equipment you need in order to take part. Etiquette, warm-up exercises and basic techniques

Although the popular conception of many martial arts is one of physical aggression, this is far from the reality which demands respect, courtesy and self-discipline.

The study of the philosophy of Shinto lies behind most martial arts disciplines.

are also included, as well as an insight into some of the weaponry that is traditionally used. If you are a more experienced martial arts practitioner, this book may introduce you to disciplines that you have not yet explored.

While some of the chapters give step-by-step instruction on how to practise some of the basic moves of the chosen discipline, there can be no substitute for learning from a professionally recognized, experienced and highly skilled teacher, who will instruct and assist you in the development of your chosen art. It is important that you train in a safe environment, that you are aware of emergency procedures in case of accidents, and that you have proper insurance cover.

There is much to be gained from learning at least a little about the many wonderful and varied martial arts and the legacies of the ancient teachers. The world of the martial arts has many doors, and, in the words of one famous Chinese proverb: "Teachers open the door but we must walk through by ourselves."

Courtesy is the foundation of martial arts. This two-handed gesture used before and after training denotes sincerity and respect.

KUNG FU

Kung fu, meaning "sustained effort or skill" incorporates hundreds of styles such as wing chun and tai chi. However, there are common traits which complement the overall picture within kung fu. All disciplines start with basic stances and motions which act as a platform from which a student may learn and study different styles and forms. As skill levels rise, these forms progress into higher levels of difficulty, allowing the student to gain fluidity and dexterity before competitive training.

功夫

WING CHUN 功夫

history *and* philosophy

Wing chun kuen kung fu is just one of many styles of martial arts, whose origins are to be found in Southern China and, compared with other martial arts, it is a relative newcomer. The term wing chun is attributed to a woman called Yim Wing Chun, who was the protégé of a Buddhist nun called Ng Mui. Wing chun is known as a "soft" style, but is in fact a blend of both "hard" and "soft" techniques. With reference to the hard concept, in simple terms this means meeting force with force, whereas the soft term refers to more evasive manoeuvres and techniques.

Roughly translated, wing chun means "beautiful spring-time" and kuen means "fist" or "fist fighting style". However, many people refer to the style as being "wing chun". This blending of hard and soft is due to the fact that it was developed by a woman and refined mainly by men. It is also said that Ng Mui once observed a battle between a snake and a crane. From her observations sprang ideas on how to develop this art. Mimicking animal movements is particularly common in Chinese martial arts.

There are many varied accounts of the history of wing chun in relation to names, dates and places. The following attempts to give one account of the history of its origin.

*The late Grand Master of wing chun kung fu, Yip Mun, uses the wooden dummy apparatus (*mook yan jong*), in order to condition both body and mind, while also improving his kung fu techniques.*

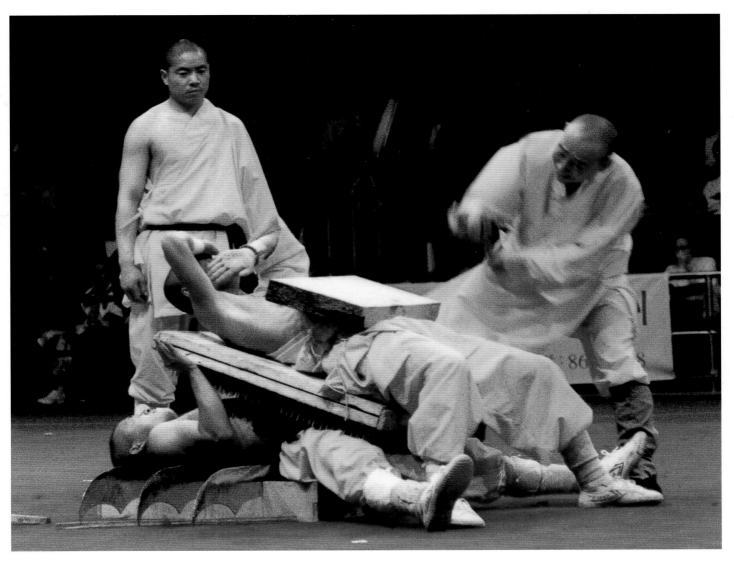

Shaolin monks demonstrate breaking techniques.

During the reign of Emperor K'anghsi of the Ching Dynasty (1662-1722), the Shaolin monastery Siu Lam of Mt Sung, in the Honan province, had become very powerful through kung fu training. The Manchurian government, fearing an uprising, sent troops to destroy Siu Lam. However, the fate of the monastery was settled internally, with traitorous monks setting it alight. Only a handful of monks and disciples managed to escape the onslaught of the Manchurian army. Among these were Abbot Chi Shin, Abbot Pak Mei, Master Fung To Tak, Master Miu Him and Abbess Ng Mui. Ng Mui was a master of Siu Lam kung fu and and became the creator of the wing chun system.

Ng Mui's ideas of close-quarter combat were totally different from the Siu Lam system of that time. She discarded many of the old traditions, which often required years of dedicated practice at each stage, and started to develop a system based on the principle of winning at all costs, by using speed and subtlety to overcome an opponent's natural advantages. Her system, as yet unnamed, therefore had less stress on muscular strength (*lik*), bone conditioning or muscular flexibility. The emphasis lay in sudden contraction and relaxation (*ging*) causing the practitioner to explode into

A stretching exercise typical of Southern Chinese martial arts.

The Zen-like appearance of the Shaolin temple evoked by nature — shaolin means small forest.

action, using natural weapons such as finger jabs to the eyes, elbow strikes to the face and the powerful use of knees and feet to an opponent's lower body.

Ng Mui later met and befriended a young, intelligent and beautiful woman named Yim Wing Chun, who was just fifteen years of age. Little is known of Yim's childhood, other than that her mother died when she was in her teens and her father, Yim Yee, was falsely accused of a crime. To avoid possible imprisonment, father and daughter moved to Mt Tai Leung, along the border of Hunan and Szechuan provinces. Here Yim soon attracted the attentions of a local landowner, Wong. He attempted to bully her into marriage and even tried to rape her. It was at the Temple on Mount Tai Leung, where Ng Mui had taken refuge, that the two women met and befriended each other.

To help protect Yim Wing Chun, Ng Mui took her into the mountains and taught her the techniques of her new fighting system, in an effort to teach her how to protect herself. Under Ng Mui's direction, Yim studied kung fu religiously, and mastered the style. Naturally, Yim Wing Chun subsequently returned to her village and defeated the bully Wong, and it is believed that Ng Mui named her new style wing chun kuen, after her protégée.

Wing chun is centred on the Taoist principle of "take the middle road". In essence, this says that you should not go to extremes, and that success is based on balance. If you are on the middle road you can see both the left and right paths, but if you venture too far to one side you may lose sight of the other. This can also be interpreted as the concept of the hard and soft principles – or *yin* and *yang*. *Yin* (the feminine side) focuses on diverting the flow of energy; *yang* (the masculine side) seeks to resist any opposing energy flow. *Yang* is primarily seen in the explosive quality of the striking moves.

Subsequent generations of wing chun practitioners have refined the system further, but always keeping to the simple, almost scientific, principles of the art: the centre-line theory (protecting and striking at the major pressure points); economy of motion (keeping every movement as simple as possible); and the self-explanatory principle of combined or simultaneous defence and attack.

BONG SAU

One of the important techniques taught in wing chun is *bong sau* (meaning "wing arm"). It is taught to beginners as a basic cover against an attack, and is particularly useful to their understanding of the style. The technique is designed to protect a wide area of your body, to yield under extreme pressure yet never allowing your arm to become trapped. It can change easily into a palm-up block and allow you to slip your hand free. The rear protective guard hand (*wu sau*) can grab and deflect the incoming strike and allow the bong to become an effective throat-cutting technique.

This *bong sau* movement demonstrates just how flexible wing chun can be. It also illustrates that if a single technique can be used in many situations, why then learn several different moves for several different situations? This reinforces the simplicity of the system.

A Shaolin monk demonstrates the flexibility that can be achieved from practising this art.

The centre-line theory is viewed as being the most definitive part of the wing chun system, since there are many attacking strikes that seek to obscure the vision of an aggressor. The centre-line is also defensive, since your own vulnerable points are protected by the counter-attacks. The practitioner is not regarded as an aggressor in a martial arts situation, because wing chun is an art of self-defence. However, if you are fighting multiple assailants, the situation may dictate the need to attack aggressively. In this type of situation, wing chun practitioners find the use of finger strikes, elbows and knee kicks to be of great value. Even the most skilled wing chun practitioner can fight only one person at a time, so the need to strike and escape is the main objective.

"Sticky hands"

One of the most important techniques in wing chun is "sticky hands" (*chi sau*). Since wing chun is a close-quarter system, it is potentially dangerous for the practitioners themselves, who are at risk of being hit, grabbed or kicked. This realization has led to a particular training method called *sheung chi sau* ("double sticky hands").

To the uninitiated, this technique is best described as a hurt boxer trying to "spoil" his opponent's moves by clinging to his arms. The aim is to prevent an opponent striking freely, giving the wing chun practitioner the opportunity to control, trap and break free to strike. The real skill lies in both parties wanting to achieve the same goal, and this has led to exceptional techniques, in which either one or both parties can train blindfolded. A skilful practitioner can eventually predict and nullify the danger.

The main areas that "sticky hands" seeks to develop fall into the categories of sensitivity, power and general fitness. Sensitivity covers such aspects as the centre-line concept, reaction to direction change, striking when the hand is freed, going with the power and not resisting force, continuous techniques (fluidity), and balance in the vertical and horizontal planes. Power involves guiding power, aggressive and explosive power, and power control and balancing-power techniques.

BENEFITS OF WING CHUN

The benefits derived from learning wing chun affect many aspects of your everyday life. These include:

- Physical and emotional control
- Confidence and well-being
- Assertiveness and reflexes
- Health improvement through physical exercise, breathing and body movement
- Comradeship
- Stress reduction
- Good posture and stability
- Mobility and flexibility

clothing *and* equipment

Practitioners of wing chun usually wear casual, clean clothing consisting of a comfortable top and trousers. Soft footwear such as slippers are worn on the feet, along with protective equipment when it is necessary, such as gum shields. There is no official grading system in wing chun, although different organizations have now developed their own systems. The sash is an integral part of clothing yet does not depict any grade. A variety of weapons is used such as butterfly knives and the 6½ point pole. The wooden dummy (*mook yan jong*) is one of the main pieces of equipment used for training in wing chun.

butterfly knives

A smartly dressed wing chun practitioner.

The wooden dummy (mook yan jong) is an impressive piece of equipment and is unique to wing chun. It is designed as a replica of the human body, in terms of the position of the torso, hands and legs, and practitioners use it to develop their blocking and striking techniques.

Etiquette

Etiquette is used as a sign of respect to the art, instructor, fellow practitioners and training area. As well as a sign of respect, the etiquette is used as a form of welcoming. The practitioner can smile when performing this ritual, as a warm friendly greeting, with no aggression intended.

SALUTATION 1

1 ◁ Stand in a relaxed position with your feet together and hands at the sides of your body. This is a formal manner of displaying etiquette in wing chun.

This etiquette is similar to the greeting used in the Chinese New Year, which commences each February, and is part of a long tradition. As a part of this tradition the fist would be fully covered as a symbol of peace.

SALUTATION 2 – *There is an alternative formality, which is characterized by a particularly friendly facial expression.*

2 △ Make a fist with your right hand and nestle it into the palm of your left hand in front of your face, approximately at chin level. Keep the fingers of your left hand pointing upwards. This shows a more informal gesture.

△ Side view of the formal etiquette, showing hand position in relation to your face. Make sure that you can still see above your hands, which should be about 10–12 in (25–30 cm) from your chin.

△ Stand as you would for the formal *rei* above, but note that the fingers of your left hand curl over the fist, partially hiding it from view. Your facial expression should be receptive and pleasant – almost like saying "hello".

Exercise | Warm-up

The following is a selection of warm-up exercises found in wing chun. In view of the close-range techniques and circular action required in certain moves, emphasis is placed on forearm power to improve strength and suppleness. Strong wrists and forearms protect the practitioner from injury upon striking and help transmit the force more effectively.

WARM-UP 1 – *This exercise is designed to make your wrists supple and increase their flexibility.*

❶ ◁ Kneel on the floor, facing forwards. Place both hands on the floor in front of you with the fingers facing backwards, towards your knees. Your back should be slightly arched. Keep looking forwards. *Note: it is the body weight on your wrists that enhances the effect of this exercise, but be careful to increase pressure gently, with practice, over a period of time.*

❷ ◁ Remain in the kneeling position and turn your right hand inwards, palm uppermost, and fingers facing towards your left arm. Gently apply pressure on the wrist, increasing the weight with practice, over a period of time. Hold for approximately 30 seconds and repeat the exercise with your left hand. Repeat 2 or 3 times.

WARM-UP 2 – *The following is a series of actions extracted from the wing chun first form* sui nim tao *designed to increase flexibility of the wrists. Perform all movements with the right hand first. This* heun sau *sequence translates as "circling hand" and is of fundamental importance to wing chun.*

❶ △ Start in a palm up position with feet a shoulder-width apart. Keep your withdrawn arm high at chest level and place your right hand, palm uppermost, in front of you. Slightly bend your elbow. Position your left fist just above your left hip. Your elbow needs to be positioned about 5 in (13 cm) from your chest. Rotate your outstretched hand in an inwards, circular motion, starting and finishing with the palm in the upwards position. Repeat 3 or 4 times and change to the left hand.

❷ △ Twist your outstretched hand inwards, with your fingers facing back towards your body. Make sure your thumb is tucked in. Your fingers need to be close together to maximize the benefit of this exercise. Hold for 10–20 seconds. From step 1 bring your fingers up and back towards the body.

❸ △ Twist your hand with an inward-turning circular action. This technique is called *fook sau* (bridge on arm). Hold for 10–20 seconds.

❹ △ Continue the *fook sau* by pushing the tips of your fingers downwards, forming part of the circular action.

❺ △ Complete the circle so the hand finishes, fingers facing upwards, with the wrist pushing in a short and powerful descent. This technique is called *jum sau*. Bring the palm back closer to the body and repeat steps 3, 4 and 5 again. Repeat as often as required.

Technique | *Kau sau*

Kau sau (circling hand or arm movement) is a popular exercise in wing chun. It is often used in demonstrations to give a "feel" for the art. It is an exercise which requires the assistance of a partner in order to develop their wing chun skills. It also seeks to develop a practitioner's evasive and striking skills.

1 ◁ The partners stand opposite each other in the ready position – both adopt frontal guard positions. Only the left practitioner is demonstrating wing chun.

2 ▷ Your partner strikes at your face with his right fist. Step back and block with your right inner arm. This technique is called *gaan sau* or "splitting block".

3 △ Circle your partner's right wrist with your defending hand and counter-attack by stepping through and striking with your left fist to your partner's short ribs.

4 ▷ Bring the low punch up and support the elbow (*tok sau*). Use both arms to pull your partner on to a low front kick. In this sequence the opponent's forwards momentum is used to your advantage.

Technique | *Chi sau*

Chi sau ("sticky hands") is one of the most famous techniques practised in wing chun. The term "sticky hands" is used to describe the continuous contact made between the two practitioners. In order to develop this technique you need to attend regular classes under professional supervision. The following steps give an insight only into the style.

❶ ◁ Stand in a relaxed fashion, opposite your partner, with your feet a shoulder-width apart and your arms in contact with your partner's forearms. Look forwards. Gently rotate your arms.

❷ ▷ Keep rotating your arms upwards and downwards, maintaining contact with your partner's forearms and wrists. You should sense a flow of energy throughout this contact.

❸ △ The practitioner on the left senses an overlap in the arms and penetrates the centre, moving from the outside left of his partner, to the outside right. He pushes through and pulls the head forwards from the back of the neck (*man geng sau*).

❹ ▷ The practitioner then follows up with an elbow strike to the face (*cup jarn*). *Note that the opponent's arms are temporarily trapped.*

Technique | Children's practice

When children practise any of the martial arts, it is very important that they receive strict and professional supervision. It is also important that they keep a good distance away from each other to prevent accidental injuries. All exercise and practice must be appropriate to the age of the child and their stage of physical and mental development.

❶ ◁ When children are practising techniques, they should stand far enough apart so that any strikes miss by between 5–8 in (13–20 cm). This is especially important when striking towards the face area.

❷ ▷ Your partner uses a left fist strike towards your face. Notice, however, that the strike finishes well short of the face.

❸ △ Defend against the attack by bringing your right arm upwards in a circular motion. The emphasis on turning the body, to avoid or redirect force, makes wing chun ideal for young people, as there is less chance of a direct strike making contact.

❹ ▷ Follow through with a right-hand striking technique to the bridge of your partner's nose. Make sure you are holding your partner's left wrist with your left hand. In this technique the practitioner has placed his fist on his partner's nose to demonstrate the striking area. When practising with movement, he would keep at a safe distance, as recommended.

Technique | *Taan sau*

Taan sau is a very typical wing chun kuen blocking move and is practised by all ages. It develops the ability, not to intercept a strike with counter-strike, but to place a cover in the way and attempt to turn. This is why blocking in wing chun kuen is often termed "bridging arms", meaning it is used to find the arm.

1 ◁ Stand opposite your partner with your feet a shoulder-width apart and both fists at the sides of your body. Bend your knees slightly and look towards your partner. This closes the inner area of the legs and ensures the groin and knees are better protected when turning. This is the basic ready position for *taan sau*, and it is important to note how close you stand to your partner.

2 ▷ Your partner uses a right fist strike towards your face, ensuring a safe distance to avoid physical contact. The closeness of the strike will be determined by experience. Maintain your posture and focus as you prepare to defend.

3 ◁ Defend against this strike by using a forward and upward open-hand block with your left hand. Keep your right hand in an open-guard position, ready to push your partner away, or prepare to either block or strike. Make sure to push the attack away by intercepting the punch as soon as possible.

4 ▷ Counter-attack by delivering a right-hand fist strike to the solar plexus. Ensure that your technique is correctly focused to avoid any injury to your partner. In this photograph the fist has made contact to demonstrate the correct target position. When actually using speed and force, it is important to maintain your focus, depending on the level of your ability.

Technique | *Rolling arm – Lok sau*

Wing chun is particularly useful for women. The fact that the founder was a woman is significant, since the close-range techniques used do not necessarily require strength or force. What is required is skill, timing and anticipation to know when a vulnerable area is available to strike. The following guide for beginners requires qualified supervision.

❷ △ Place your right hand on your partner's right arm ready to twist and turn (*laap sau* means deflecting arm).

❶ △ Face your partner with your feet a shoulder-width apart, keep your back straight and look forwards. Your hands should be forward and forearms in contact with your partner. This is the ready position for *lok sau* practice.

❸ △ Maintain a rolling action that delivers a certain amount of pressure on your partner.

4 ◁ The technique has now completely reversed from the beginning.

5 △ As in step 2, move on to perform the same technique, taking you back to step 1. You will find the technique alternating between you and your partner.

6 △ You now change sides to perform an alternative to continuing to roll back and forth with your arms. As you feel your partners desire to deflect your arm, take hold of their arm and deliver a right punch. Your partner, feeling the grab, responds by blocking the incoming strike through performing a left *bong sau*.

7 ▷ The sequence now follows through as in steps 1–4. Whenever there is an attempt to deflect the strike, the other side has a chance to grab and change sides. This sequence develops good reaction to grabs, punches and change of direction. This technique can be developed to an extremely high speed with the correct supervision and lots of practice.

Technique | *Mook yan jong*

Wooden dummy practice (*mook yan jong*) is used to develop various blocks and strikes. It represents the human body and was invented by Ng Mui as she stood by a well collecting water. It is a unique piece of equipment found only in the art of wing chun and it plays an integral part in a practitioner's development of the techniques.

◁ Demonstrates a low kick used to break an opponent's stance.

▽ Demonstrates a sweep kick and counter-strike.

◁ Demonstrates a double-palm push known as *po pai jeung*.

▷ A complex movement called *gaan sau*, meaning "splitting block".

Many of the weapons in wing chun have developed from everyday practical tools and familiar objects used in farming, such as rice flails, or boating, such as poles and staffs, which were used to carry water to and from wells. These are common to nearly all Chinese martial arts.

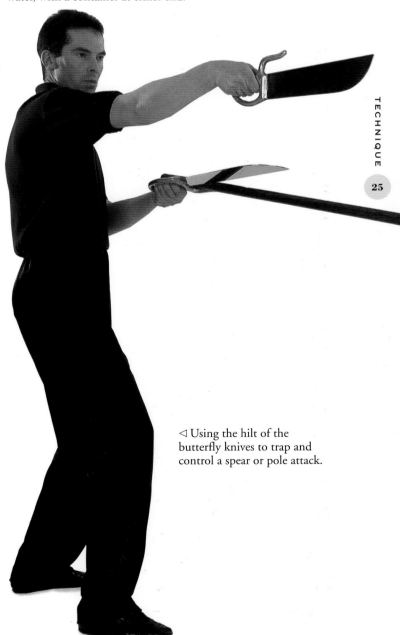

◁ The first weapon to be demonstrated is the *luk dim boon kwun*, an 8 ft (2.5 m) length of sturdy, tapering wood, known as the 6½ point pole. This refers to the six main movements where the pole is used to block and strike, as well as small half movements. It is tapered at one end to prevent it becoming excessively heavy and allow the tip to be moved faster. The pole derives from the similar object that the boat people used to push their boats away from the bank. It was also used for carrying water, with a container at either end.

△ The butterfly knives being used for "trapping the spear".

△ A deflective movement known as *laap do*.

◁ Using the hilt of the butterfly knives to trap and control a spear or pole attack.

MOK-GAR

功夫

history *and* philosophy

Shaolin mok-gar kuen is one of the original family disciplines of kung fu, from Southern China, and is well-known for its kicking techniques. Practitioners are not restricted just to kicking, however, since the use of a full range of weapons is also part of the system. The resulting flexibility of attack and defence epitomizes the original concept of Chinese martial arts: to express yourself fully in the attempt to triumph in combat. When engaging in combat, the objective is to win, so practitioners believe that to place any restrictions on one particular movement would be to put themselves at a disadvantage.

Shaolin mok-gar kuen, so legend has it, was originally developed by a midget called Mok-Da-Si, in the Shaolin monastery in Southern China. He taught this style, known then as shaolin chuen, to his family in the Tong-Kwun district of Kwong-Tong province, and the name was retained until the third generation, when it was renamed mok-gar (after Mok's family).

The style has passed virtually unchanged through many generations, and is still faithfully taught today, according to its original concept. Indeed, it shares the same good reputation with four other contemporary Southern Chinese family styles: hung-gar, choi-gar, lee-gar and lau-gar. Each family

The spirit of kung fu is often reflected within the face and poise of Asian temple guardians.

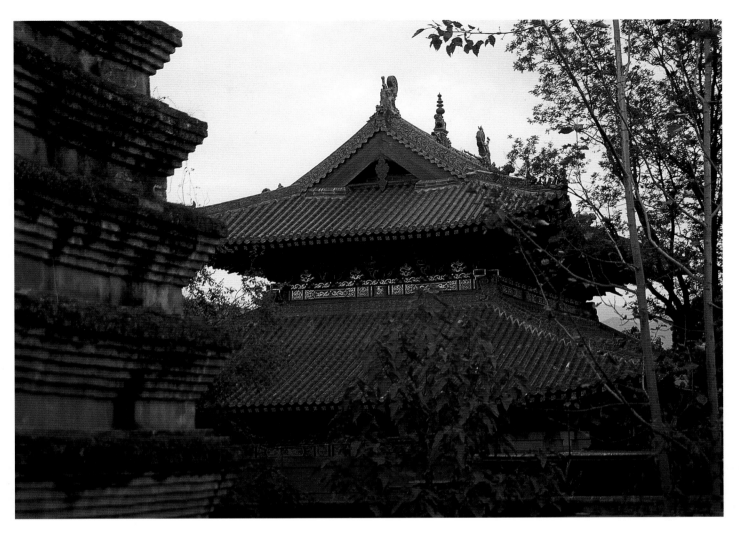

The elegant roof of a Shaolin temple with ornate wood carvings.

The training stumps upon which Shaolin monks would stand to improve their skills of balance and one-on-one harmony.

became well-known for its specific strength within the style. The Chinese have a traditional saying, which when translated, calls to mind the strong points of these styles: "Hung's fists, mok's kicks and lee's staff."

Mok-gar kuen practice traditionally involves the use of two wooden dummies. One is called *mook-yan-jong*, with projections which resemble arms, and is used for blocking and countering. The other is called *darn gee* and is particular to mok-gar. The *darn gee* consists of a hollow bamboo post 13 ft (4 m) high and 4 in (10 cm) in diameter, which is set into the ground by about 3 ft (1 m). It is filled with washers (originally coins) and is used to practise all of the attacks necessary for a student to learn. This training is excellent for building physical power and developing effective punches and kicks. This is important in mok-gar, since every student has to pass through a stage where he or she develops a considerable amount of power before progressing.

One of the unique training drills found in mok-gar kuen is that of the *darn gee* kicking technique. In kung fu, each school has its own method of teaching the kicks using various mechanical facilities. Irrespective of the method, the aim is the same: to increase the freedom of leg movements, enhance speed, improve accuracy, and to develop and harden the soles of the feet.

During the course of training, the *darn gee* helps practitioners to improve their stamina, hardness, speed, accuracy

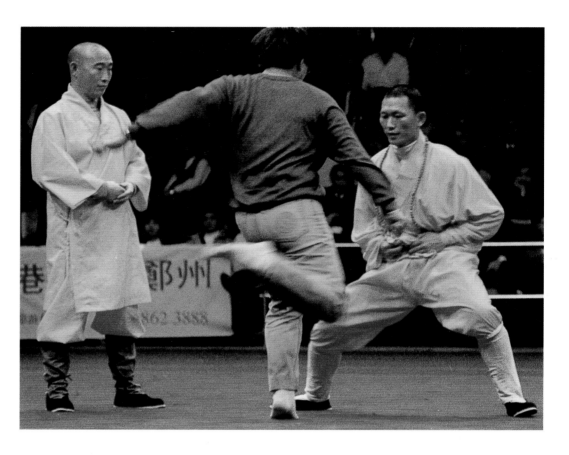

Well-known for its kicking techniques, mok-gar kuen kung fu also teaches how to withstand being kicked. Here a Shaolin monk is totally open to a vicious groin kick.

and strength in kicking techniques. This unique training drill is a stage that all mok-gar practitioners must experience if they wish to develop a high standard within this style. The 108 movements that are the basis of the mok-gar style can be used in many ways, from just a single punch, which may be all that is needed to win a fight, to multiple jumping kicks.

When experienced, students progress to learning a soft form of kung fu, called tai chi. Sifu Chan, who came to England to develop the system which incorporated the use of weapons, teaches the wu style tai chi, based on the Taoist symbol of yin and yang (soft and hard). Tai chi teaches you to be aware of, and to react to, any form of attack, and to be ever-changing and formless. To learn and combine these two systems of kung fu is not an easy task, but once acquired, the knowledge and experience can prove invaluable.

Madame Mok Kwei Lan

Madame Mok Kwei Lan, known as the Tigress, was only a teenager when she started giving kung fu instruction some sixty years ago. Madame Mok was a native of Kao Yao, a small town near Canton. As a child, she was taught the family art of mok-gar kung fu – known as "Snapping the Iris" – by her uncle. In the face of strong disapproval – women were not encouraged to learn martial arts – she continued to study secretly with her uncle, by whom she was eventually adopted, with her parents' approval. She eventually married her uncle's friend, Wong Fei Hung, whom she assisted by

looking after his gymnasium, giving kung fu instruction and practising as a trained osteopath.

There are many stories regarding Madame Mok, as the Tigress, being challenged to fight. One particular incident occurred after she had moved to Hong Kong and was living in the Wanchai district. Once, when buying food in the marketplace, Madame Mok saw four men bullying a fishmonger. As she intervened to help him, the four men turned on her and attacked her with poles. She then proceeded to take away all of the men's weapons and knocked the aggressors down one by one. The four attackers ran away in great pain, as the onlookers clapped with delight. Stories regarding this incident spread far and wide, enhancing her already formidable reputation.

BENEFITS OF MOK-GAR KUEN

The benefits derived from learning mok-gar kuen affect many aspects of your everyday life. These include:

- Flexibility and durability
- Confidence and assertiveness
- Stamina and fitness
- Health and well-being
- Comradeship
- Stress reduction

The ability to defend oneself against an armed attacker is the mark of a competent and assured mok-gar kuen practitioner.

Demonstrating a technique to a group of students.

clothing *and* equipment

In general, practitioners of mok-gar wear a white T-shirt, which may or may not depict black writing showing the name of the art and training area, together with black trousers. Instructors may wear red trousers. It is also permissible for instructors to wear a white mandarin jacket. Trainers (sneakers) or bare feet are permissible during the practice of mok-gar. Weapons in mok gar include the three-sectional staff, spear, staff, split staff, *siu so gee, tee-chec, dip do* (butterfly knives), *guay*, pegs, broad sword, tai chi sword, three-section and nine-section steel whip.

white mandarin top

trousers

sashes

3-section staff

siu so gee

black sash

slippers

dip do knives

broad sword

4 red-banded sash

red sash

SASH GRADING

Instructors wear a black sash and practitioners wear the following:

Novices

yellow sash	1st grade
orange sash	2nd grade
green sash	3rd grade
blue sash	4th grade
brown sash	5th grade
black sash	1st degree

Once a practitioner has achieved the black sash, they progress in degrees, which starts at one red band per degree. After achieving 10th degree they can wear a red sash.

Etiquette

The sign of respect in mok-gar is manifested as a "salute" by practitioners. It is performed at the beginning and end of every session to demonstrate that the practitioner is following the true Shaolin way (having the right attitude and respect towards the art and its beliefs).

❶ ◁ Stand in a relaxed position with your hands behind your back. There are no specific rules governing which hand should be over which − it is just a natural standing posture with feet facing forwards, a shoulder-width apart, back straight, shoulders relaxed and eyes looking forwards.

△ Rear view of hand positions.

❷ △ Make a fist with your right hand and keep your left hand open with your thumb relaxed. Place your fist into the centre of the palm of your left hand and prepare to move forwards.

❸ △ Step forwards with your left foot into the cat stance. At the same time, continue to bring your hands round to the centre of your upper body.

❹ △ Side view of the salute position.
Note: this salute is also used before sparring, as a sign of respect to your partner. Following the etiquette, practitioners stand in a relaxed position with their hands behind their back, as depicted in step 1.

Exercise | Warm-up

As with the other disciplines, mok-gar uses a variety of warm-up routines which are designed to prevent injuries during practice. Since this discipline is predominantly centred around leg techniques, leg-stretching exercises are particularly important, focusing on leg muscles, ligaments and tendons.

WARM-UP 1 – *Stretching the leg tendons and hamstring muscles is a vital part of the warm-up.*

WARM-UP 2 – *This exercise stretches the inner thighs and develops good body posture.*

❶ ◁ Raise your leg as high as is comfortable. Gradually build up the tempo and height of the kick. Each exercise is performed by counting from one to ten in Cantonese. Then change to the other leg.

▽ A variation of the front-kick stretching exercise is to kick your leg forwards and outwards in a circular motion. Try to keep the heel of your stationary leg firmly planted on the ground while kicking. If you go up on to your toes you will lose balance. Don't worry about achieving any great height with any kicking or stretching exercise if you are just starting out – it is better to aim for waist level and gradually build up the height.

▽ Take hold of your left foot with your left hand and bring it in towards your body and then out towards your left side. This is not an easy exercise for beginners. Only go as high as is comfortable.

WARM-UP 3 – *Breathing exercises play an important part in mok-gar. The following exercise demonstrates what is known as dynamic tension, which is a body tensing exercise.*

◁ Lower your body into the horse stance, knees bent and with your feet facing forwards. Breathe in slowly through your nose, right down into the pit of your stomach. Hold this for a few seconds and then breathe out slowly through your mouth. While breathing, move both hands in a circular action, first forwards, then back in towards you, finally pushing out to the sides.

WARM-UP 4 – *When exercising with a partner, take great care not to stretch him too far. Apply the exercise gently, gradually pushing the leg a little further each time you practise.*

△ Lie down on the floor and allow your partner to secure your right knee and raise your left leg. Keep your leg straight. Your partner then pushes your left leg upwards. Change to the opposite leg and repeat the exercise 3 or 4 times each side.

WARM-UP 5 – *This series of moves is designed to develop your arms.*

❶ △ Gently make contact with your partner's forearms in a rotating action, first left, then right.

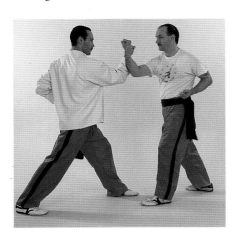

❷ △ Bend your arms so that you are now making contact with your partner's upturned fists in line with your chin. As you perform this exercise, try to use hip rotation to enhance the technique.

❸ △ Lower your arms so that you are making contact with the lower part of your partner's forearms. This looks very similar to the first position.

Technique | One-man blocking

The purpose of this technique is to develop basic blocking forms. Each movement is a block towards an on-coming attack. Beginners would learn these basics before starting to work with a partner. The second stage involves the two-man blocking form to develop awareness, timing, distancing and body movement.

❶ ◁ Stand in a natural position with your feet together and both fists at your side.

❷ △ Keeping your toes together, move your heels outwards.

❸ △ Twist on the balls of your feet and then twist your heels as you move into a wider stance. Straighten your toes as you then move outwards.

❹ △ Continue to pivot on your heels and toes into a low horse stance. Keep both knees bent. It is important to push your knees outwards.

❺ △ Raise your right hand into an upper block position. Keep your left fist and elbow tucked into your side. Look straight ahead and repeat this exercise with the left arm.

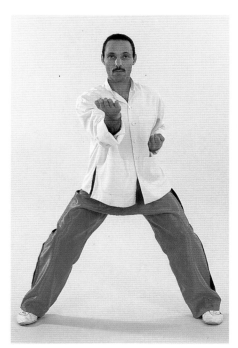

❻ △ Push your right arm forwards with your right palm moving forwards and upwards. Keep your left fist on your left hip in preparation to move forwards. Ensure you are still in a low horse stance.

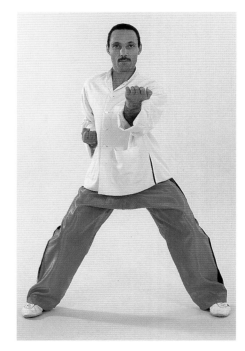

❼ △ Repeat the exercise with your left arm and follow through with your right. It is important to keep your back straight and maintain the same posture.

8 △ With an open right palm, prepare to block across your body.

9 △ Follow through with a downwards, circular block to your right side. Repeat these moves, reversing hand and arm positions.

10 △ Push both hands forwards, palms upwards and thumbs tucked in.

11 △ Rotate your hands in a circular motion towards your face, keeping your little fingers together to start the rotation movement.

△ The rolling-finger technique seen from the side view.

12 △ Continue to rotate the hands so that they move into the tiger-claw position.

13 △ Defend with your left hand crossing your body. Keep your right hand on your hip and maintain the low horse stance.

14 △ Move your hands into the butterfly position, by crossing your right palm over your left, in preparation to push downwards.

15 △ Push your hand down, keeping your right hand on top.

16 △ Both hands need to be flat as they push down in a circular action. Note the low body position. Ensure your right hand is on top of your left hand, with fingers straight. Draw your left leg up to your right leg and bring your fists back to your waist to finish – this is similar to the starting position.

Technique | Two-man blocking form

The two-man defence form is designed to develop effective blocking and striking techniques. The advantage of using a partner is to promote increased awareness of movement, timing and delivery of the block. Such practice sharpens the ability to focus on a moving target and develop a "feel" for when and how to defend and strike.

1 △ Lower your posture and transfer 70 per cent of your weight on to your back leg. Slightly bend your front knee and keep your toes turned slightly inwards. Place your hands in the guard position with your right hand open. *Note: you can use either hand, depending on the fighting posture adopted.*

2 △ Your opponent delivers a strike to your face. Deflect the attack using an upper-arm block with your left arm. The front arm must always be in a fist position with the rear in an open hand guard.

3 △ Bring your arm back in to your body and bring your left leg up in preparation to strike your opponent in the floating rib.

4 △ Deliver a kick to the floating rib. Ensure that it is the heel of your foot that makes contact, otherwise your kick will be weak and you could hurt your toes. Maintain a good posture and keep looking at your opponent.

Technique | Drilling stance

The drilling stance exercise is designed to improve overall general fitness, flexibility, balance and strength. Regular practice enhances leg mobility and coordination of movement and breathing in preparation to perform many of the skills utilized in mok-gar, including *kata* and weaponry. Repetition is viewed as important in all basic practice.

❶ △ Lower your body into the horse stance and place both fists on your hips. Maintain a low posture and keep looking forwards.

❷ △ Turn to the left and move into the bow stance – so called because it echoes the shape of a bow and arrow. Place the fists out forwards (natural, relaxed breathing ensures that the practitioner exhales on the strike). Return to the horse stance and repeat the exercise to the opposite side. Repeat 2 or 3 times each side.

❸ △ Move through with your right leg into a forward cat position. Keep your knees well-bent with about 70 per cent of your weight on your rear leg. Your hands should be in the claw style – known as the tiger claw movement. Repeat, moving to your right side.

Technique | Self-defence

Mok-gar utilizes many of the basic techniques and forms into effective self defence applications. The following demonstrates one such application, showing the use of body blocks, hand strikes and leg techniques. Various combination techniques are practised in mok-gar to defend against a variety of attacks to the head and body.

1 △ Use a lower-forearm block as your opponent moves in with his right hand to strike at your upper body.

2 △ Take hold of your opponent's right wrist with your right hand.

3 △ Bring your left hand up in a circular inwards and outwards motion, aiming to strike the aggressor's nose with the back of your knuckles. At this point the aggressor should be disorientated, enabling you to either escape or to further restrain him.

▷ An alternative defensive strike would be to utilize your legs, making contact with the knife edge of your foot. Mok-gar is well-known for its front kicking strikes (sickle kicks).

ADVANCED
Technique | Weapons

Mok-gar utilizes a variety of weapons, many of which are unique to the art, and were adapted from agricultural tools. They were used by farmers to protect their family and land. Today, these weapons are used to maintain the tradition of mok-gar, which practitioners learn as they progress through the art, and they are seen as an extension of the hand.

TEE CHEC – metal sai

△This is a classical pose using the *tee chec*. Here, a block and striking action, taken from a *mok-gar* form (a set of pre-designed moves), is being illustrated.

PEGS – two small rounded pieces of wood

△This weapon gets its name of "the peg" because of its similarity to a wooden dowel. The pegs are principally used to strike at an aggressor's vulnerable spots, such as the mandible, limbs and pressure points.

DIP DO – butterfly knives

△ Illustrating the *dip do* (butterfly knives).

SIU SO GEE – two pieces of wood joined together by a metal chain

△ This shows the *siu so gee* in action. The history of the *siu so gee* begins with a legend that an unknown instructor broke one of his favourite fighting sticks. He was so attached to this particular weapon that he continued to use it, even though it was broken. In this way he developed the shorter stick into a weapon in its own right. The *siu so gee* is sometimes referred to as the "little sweeper".

△ Demonstrating the *siu so gee* as an effective blocking weapon.

THREE-SECTION STAFF – *This was developed as a battlefield weapon and proved particularly useful against cavalry.*

▷ The three-section staff is a complex weapon to use, but very effective in both close and long-range combat. When fully extended it has a 9 ft (2.75 m) range. At close quarters, it can be used for choking and striking, as well as for hooking other weapons to disarm an opponent.

KICK BOXING 功夫

history *and* philosophy

Kick boxing is a relatively modern martial arts system, whose syllabus was derived by combining several fighting techniques from a variety of the more traditional disciplines, including kung fu, kyokushinkai karate, Thai boxing, kyokky shinkai and tae kwondo.

Martial arts boomed during the early 1970s and interest was greatly increased by their emphasis on competition fighting. Chinese styles of fighting began to take on a more Westernized form in the UK, and even more so in the United States, where the first real freestyle systems were beginning to be developed. Indeed, many people claim that kick boxing originated in the US during the 1970s. This, they say, was due to various American karate practitioners becoming frustrated with the limitations of tournament competitive scoring. While karate and the other disciplines were viewed as being entrenched with theories and set *kata*,

Training with hand-held equipment and protective gear is essential if practitioners plan to take their skill into the ring.

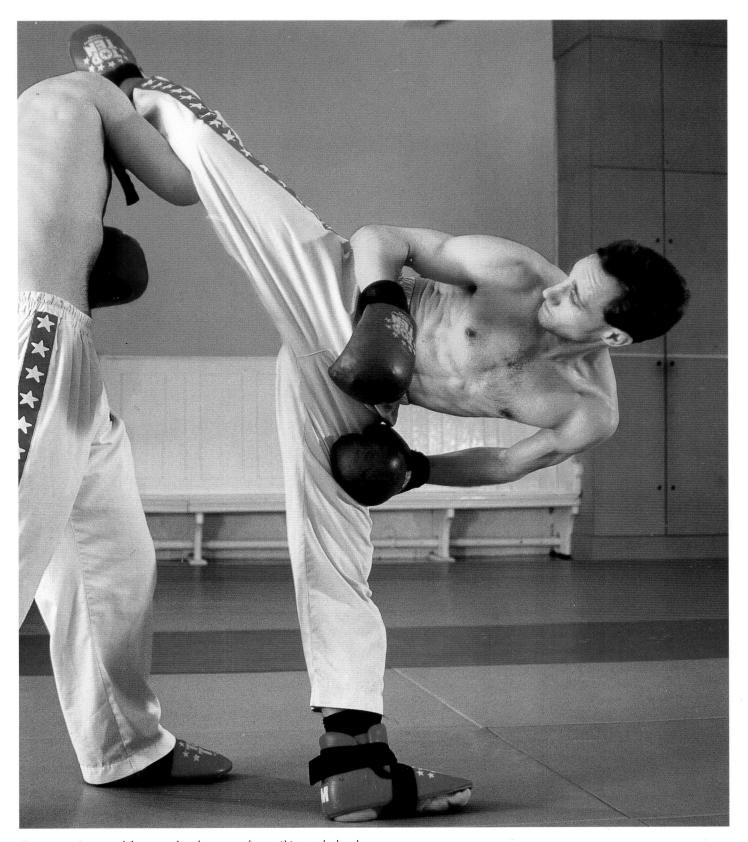

Demonstrating superb leg control and posture when striking to the head.

and were performed in a controlled environment, practitioners wanted to see how effective their moves would be in a more realistic environment. Great emphasis began to be placed on specialized techniques, such as kicks and punches, being delivered with full force. Although full-contact karate was already established, concerns were expressed for the safety of competitors. The first tournament stars of kick boxing were Bill "Superfoot" Wallis, Demetrius Havanas, Joe Lewis, Jeff Smith and Benny Urquidez.

Initially, some people felt that kick boxing looked amateurish, and questioned its validity as a traditional martial art. It is viewed by many as a sport that is a relatively

As with conventional boxing, full contact kick boxing tournaments are conducted in a boxing ring environment.

new discipline and has yet to establish long-term traditions and history.

The World Kick Boxing Association (known as the WKA) apparently came into being in the early 1970s following a tournament with Benny Urquidez, who was sent to Japan to represent America in a kick boxing championship. He won his first world title in 1974. Although many other kick boxing representatives were defeated, Urquidez was able to hold his own, and he was successful to some extent because of his research into Eastern training methods and his well-developed boxing and judo skills. One memorable bout was against the renowned Fujiwara, who was skilled in both karate and Thai boxing.

There is a close affinity between kick boxing and Thai boxing. While it is believed that the Americans had created this concept in their attempt to find a sport that could refine full-contact competition, it is believed that the development of kick boxing was borne out of the WKA finding common ground between Eastern and Western fighting culture.

It is also believed that Joe Cawley and Don and Judy Quinn, along with Howard Hansen, a shorin ryu karate black belt, were the initial promoters of kick boxing and worked together for improved recognition. Hansen took kick boxing a stage further, by introducing fights in a boxing ring, rather than the usual karate tournament bouts. He became known as a ring matchmaker, staging a variety of successful events with such stars as Bill "Superfoot" Wallis.

New rules evolved and were introduced into kick boxing, most notably weight divisions – from fly weight to heavy weight – similar to those in orthodox boxing.

A down-side to the discipline in those early days was criticism of a high risk of injury. This led to improvement in the safety rules, such as contestants wearing protective clothing to cushion the impact of blows. When wearing protective clothing, there are two main fighting distinctions: semi-contact and full contact.

Semi-contact is where two fighters are allowed "reasonable", light contact in an attempt to score points off each other, in the same way as fencing. Full contact is usually fought under the same conditions as a standard boxing match, in which a knock-out is the ultimate aim. Individual clubs compete at inter-club competitions or in open, national

Protective clothing or not, care and caution are always of paramount importance.

In Thailand many fights end this way!

and international, martial arts tournaments. Women do not generally compete against men, but women's kick boxing competitions are becoming more common.

Rules vary, but more recently tournament organizers have insisted on competitors wearing full protective clothing, for even in "semi-contact with control" bouts, injuries can still occur. Men are expected to wear a head guard, gum shield, groin guard, shin, hand and foot pads. Women are expected to wear the same, except that the groin guard is swapped for a chest guard. These rules apply to children.

The order of belts (representing degrees of proficiency) are: white, yellow, orange, blue, green, purple, brown and black. Once the black-belt level has been achieved, progression to a higher grade is through degrees of *dan*, signified by a stripe in the belt – for example, a 1st-*dan* practitioner is entitled to wear a black belt containing one stripe.

Although traditional moves are not really taught, there are set moves that practitioners need to acquire in order to attain each belt. These include hand and kick blocks, shadow boxing, sparring, kicks, punches and wood breaking.

Caution: any breaking techniques must be supervised by an instructor. Never try to perform breaking techniques without professional guidance, as serious injury may result. Injuries may be immediate or take years to become apparent, but the risk is very real. It is an aggressive sport, but as with most other martial arts disciplines, the true kick boxer is less likely to initiate or be involved in violence, preferring to walk away from a difficult situation.

BENEFITS OF KICK BOXING

There are numerous benefits derived from learning kick boxing, which extend into many aspects of everyday life. These include:

- Appeals to both men and women, irrespective of occupation or level of fitness
- Develops strength and flexibility
- Improves mental agility and stamina
- Powerful and skilful sport
- Increases confidence
- Promotes fitness and well-being
- Reduces stress
- Promotes comradeship
- Assists with self-defence skills

clothing *and* equipment

The clothing of kick boxing practitioners can vary from club to club. Designs are similar and usually consist of a comfortable top and elasticated trousers. Any colour is acceptable. In view of the emphasis on controlled fighting (sparring), it is very important to wear protective clothing and equipment. Protective equipment must be checked regularly to prevent any unnecessary injury to either the practitioner or their partner.

Loose cotton top, which will depict the colours of the style and club.

Elasticated trousers, which are usually white or black with a stripe identifying the style and club.

ORDER OF KICK BOXING GRADES	
Beginner	White
Beginner	Yellow
Junior	Orange
Junior	Green
Intermediate	Blue
Intermediate	Purple
Senior	Brown
1st degree	Black
2nd degree	Black
3rd degree	Black

Protective head-guard and gloves for full contact sparring. The head-guard must fit securely.

Padded footwear to protect both the practitioner and his/her partner during kicking strikes.

Etiquette

Etiquette in kick boxing is used at the beginning of a practice session, when training with a partner and when competing in a tournament. As with other disciplines, the style and form of the etiquette is used as a sign of respect towards your partner or opponent. There is only one bow, as shown.

READY POSITION

1 ◁ Stand with an upright posture – back straight and eyes looking forward. Ensure your shoulders are relaxed and stomach muscles firm. Turn your hands into fists by curling the fingers (starting with the little finger). Place your thumb securely on top of your fingers and position both hands in front of your body. Make sure your elbows are tucked in and feet comfortably astride. Bend both knees slightly and keep your elbows close in to your waist, to ensure there are no vulnerable areas where an opponent could strike. Maintain an inner calm while adopting an assertive, well-focused attitude towards your training partner.

2 ◁ Lower your body, keeping your elbows well tucked in. Perform a bow at about 30 degrees without taking your eyes off your partner.

FIGHTING STANCE

▽ Move forwards from the ready position, using your preferred leg and with your fists raised. Keep your elbows close to your body and your fists clenched. Keep your guard up in front of your body as a protective measure, to deflect or strike, as required. In this side view you can see the correct upright posture and the angle of the fists. Fists that are too high increase the vulnerability of your lower body; if they are too low, your face is at risk. The centre-body position offers the best overall protection.

Exercise | Warm-up

Exercises in kick boxing are designed to improve stamina and enhance flexibility, working towards the goal of toning and strengthening the body and increasing mental agility. Below is a selection of the more important exercises used in warm-up sessions, prior to basic practice. There is particular emphasis on leg stretching and stamina building.

WARM-UP 1 – *This exercise is excellent for stretching the spine and increasing general flexibility.*

❶△ Lie down on a flat, comfortable surface and slightly raise your knees off the floor. Place your hands at the side of your head.

❷△ Keeping your hands lightly at the side of your head, raise your torso while pulling your knees up and into your chest. Lie back down without letting your feet or head touch the ground and repeat 4 or 5 times.

WARM-UP 2 – *This exercise is called the horse-riding stance, because of its obvious resemblance to a figure seated on a horse. It is intended to strengthen buttocks, inner thighs, triceps and biceps.*

WARM-UP 3 – *This exercise needs to be performed slowly and gently, to allow yourself to become supple naturally . It stretches and strengthens the hamstrings and needs to be practised regularly.*

△ With your legs stretched fairly wide, bend your knees while keeping your back straight. Thrust your left fist out in front of your body in a striking position and place your right fist on your hip, touching your waistline. Hold this position for about 60–90 seconds. Alternate with your opposite fist and repeat 4 or 5 times.

△ Let your partner take hold of your leg at the ankle and gently raise it, stopping periodically to ensure you are comfortable. Your partner, in an upright position, needs to gently raise your leg. Keep a straight back leg and upright posture. Hold for 20–30 seconds and repeat 3 to 4 times each side.

WARM-UP 4 — *It is important to perform this exercise sensibly, with both partners working together. You will cause unnecessary pain if you push down too heavily, without regard for your partner's level of flexibility.*

WARM-UP 5 — *This exercise assists in strengthening both the stomach muscles and lower back of both practitioners. Mutual cooperation is important to ensure maximum benefit and safety.*

△ Lie on your back and place your hands either at the sides of your body or lightly on your stomach. Let your legs fall apart and keep your breathing slow and calm. Your partner then gently pushes down on your inner thighs, stretching your legs apart, for approximately 60 seconds.

△ Lie on your back and bring your knees into your chest. Place your hands, palms down, on the floor at your sides (experienced people may prefer to rest their hands on their thighs). Allow your standing partner to lean forwards at 45 degrees, resting her stomach on the soles of your feet with hands clasped behind her back. Both partners need to keep the stomach muscles tense. Hold for 20–30 seconds and swop positions. As your strength increases, extend the exercise period, staying within the limits of what feels comfortable to you.

WARM-UP 6 — *This exercise seeks to strengthen the upper body muscles through the application of mild resistance against your partner's applied reasonable pressure.*

WARM-UP 7 — *This wheelbarrow press-up is an advanced exercise for more experienced practitioners. It is good for developing the top part of the body, including the triceps, biceps and abdomen.*

△ Lie face down on the floor in a press-up position with feet together, hands flat and back straight. With your partner's hands on your shoulder applying gentle downward pressure, push your body up by straightening your elbows. Relax for a few seconds after each press-up. Repeat the exercise no more than 5 times in a session. Change roles and repeat.

△ Go into the usual press-up position and then let your partner take hold of and raise your ankles to waist level. Push down to perform the press-ups, ensuring maximum pressure on the upper part of your body, while your partner continues to hold your legs by the ankles. Then lower your body towards the floor and do not let your face make contact with the ground. Push down as near to the floor as you can. Finally, push your body up from the floor as high as you can and then clap your hands before going back down. Perform this exercise fairly slowly and no more than 10 times.

COMBINATION
Technique | Self-defence

Many people take up a martial art as a self-defence measure. Kick boxing utilizes various self-defence moves, and the following technique is just one example of the many strategies that are suitable for both men and women, when seeking to learn self-protection. Physical defence is only used as a last resort, when all else has failed.

1 ◁ Stand in the ready position with your fists at waist level. Your opponent adopts a fighting posture.

2 ▷ Your opponent moves in with a side-kicking attack.

3 ◁ You move 45 degrees to the right (away from the kicking leg) and then move back in with a hooking block. This is immediately followed by a punch to either the upper body or head region.

△ The close-up view shows how the hooking block works. This is achieved by using a scooping motion to sweep the attacking leg, and then control the opponent's body, by immediately securing the leg in towards your body. This puts the opponent in a very vulnerable position, where it is difficult for him to maintain balance with only one foot in the air.

4▽ You can now perform a leg sweep to unbalance your opponent by bringing your right leg around his leg. *Note: it is important to continue securing the opponent's right leg to maintain control of the technique. This technique is only used in self-defence practice.*

CAUTION
Always gently lower your partner to the floor, especially if you are practising with minimum protection. When fully protected and on a matted floor, experienced people can practise break-falling techniques. In a real self-defence situation, hard strikes could be applied such as to the face, body or groin. However, it is important to be aware of your legal rights concerning the use of "reasonable force".

◁ This close-up shows your hand position on your opponent's shoulder, ready to push him forwards and downwards on to the floor. It is important to hold on to your opponent when practising this technique, by taking hold of his clothing on the right or left shoulder.

5◁ Once your opponent is on the floor, start to move your head and body to the side and out of reach, so that you cannot be grabbed and pulled to the floor. Maintain a good stance and posture to help you avoid losing your balance and falling down with your opponent.

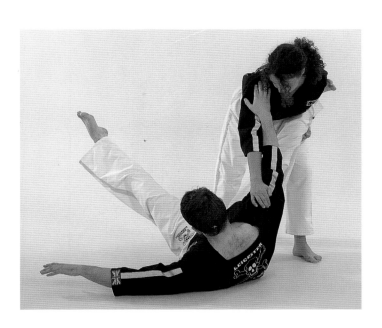

6▷ A variety of finishing techniques can be applied, ranging from punching to kicking. Ideally a kicking technique is useful, as it enables you to maintain a safer distance.

Technique | Contact sparring

Contact sparring is a fundamental element of kick boxing. Respect and control of the techniques is of paramount importance, to maintain safety. It is commonplace for men and women to practise with each other, although in the competition environment sexes are usually demarcated. The following demonstrates one basic routine.

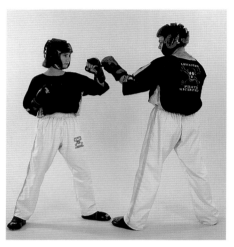

❶ △ Stand opposite your partner, making sure you maintain focus. Keep your guard up and your feet a shoulder-width apart. An inner sense of assertion and control is vital. Stand about one and a half arm's length away from your partner, in readiness to commence sparring. If you are too close you increase your vulnerability to being punched or kicked.

❷ △ Perform a bow by lowering the top part of your body by about 30 degrees. Maintain your guard by keeping your eyes fixed on your partner.

❸ △ Move into fighting posture by touching gloves. This is a sign of respect, indicating that although you intend to go into a fighting situation, you are still showing sportsmanship and friendship.

❺ △ If you manage to block a kick or punch, try to score a point by punching the body or head region.

❹ △ The object of the sparring is to increase speed and agility. As one partner may try to score a point with a kick, the other must try to block. Note the good upright posture when kicking and the guard being kept in place in preparation for a counter-attack.

COMPETITION TECHNIQUES

It is important that you use the correct protective equipment – head padding, body armour, shin, hand and foot protection – in competition. Both partners will wear gum shields, and men must wear groin guards and women chest guards. It is very important that you show respect towards your partner. Sparring should not be seen as an opportunity to hurt somebody.

The following examples demonstrate a variety of close punching techniques. A particular style of punching in kick boxing is the uppercut punch. It is important to practise these techniques under proper supervision from a qualified instructor, and while wearing the correct protective clothing.

❶ ◁ A round-house hook to the side of the head. This technique demonstrates an effective strike to a vulnerable area of the head e.g. hinge of jaw (mandible) and therefore warrants points.

❷ ▷ An uppercut to the chin. This strike has to be delivered at close range and could follow a number of other striking techniques. As with all striking techniques which make contact, an opening has been created, either by the partner letting his guard down, or their position inviting an opportunity to strike at a vulnerable area.

❸ ▽ A straight punch to the body. As your partner's guard has moved, a vulnerable area has been exposed, which creates an opportunity to strike the solar plexus or stomach region, for example.

CAUTION
Whilst partners wear protective equipment, a degree of caution is still exercised through the sensible application of punching techniques. Remember: when sparring, partners are moving around, which requires skills in distancing and focusing. It is easy to hit an accessible partner, and therefore the skill lies in effective control and discipline of movement.

Technique | Blocking

As part of defensive manoeuvres, blocking plays an important role. The following demonstrates a variety of blocking techniques which can be employed against different attacks. Leg movements feature predominantly in kick boxing and are difficult to block, as the legs are the most powerful striking tool.

△ A double-handed block to defend against a kick to the body.

△ An open-handed block to defend against a circular leg strike.

△ A defence against a head attack, using an upper block.

△ An outward-hooking block to a leg attack.

The following demonstrates some of the kicking techniques that can be included in competition and in advanced practice. The top two pictures display kicks that can score points in competition fighting, while the two pictures along the bottom demonstrate more advanced techniques that are not usually allowed in competition sparring.

△ A head kick being counter-attacked by an upper-head block.

△ A spinning back kick into the solar plexus region.

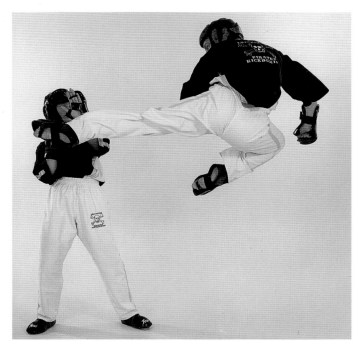

△ A flying side kick, known as a "jump or flying technique", achieved by jumping, turning and kicking your partner while in mid air. A jump kick is to the body while a flying kick is to the head.

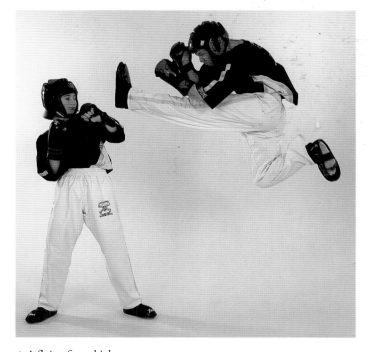

△ A flying front kick.

SCORES

In competition, points are awarded for particular techniques, with extra points being scored for more complicated and difficult manoeuvres such as combination techniques.

Points can vary, but the standard scoring system is usually:

one point for a hand technique to the body or head

two points for a leg technique to the body

three points for a leg technique to the head.

TAE KWONDO

태
권
도

It is widely believed that a Buddhist monk named Won Qwang originated the five principles – etiquette, modesty, perseverance, self-control and indomitable (invincible) spirit – that today form the basis of tae kwondo. This art is renowned for its exceptional kicking and jumping techniques. It is viewed not only as an extremely effective self-defence system, but is also a very popular international sport. Early training involves simple punching and blocking techniques, which many may also relate to karate.

TAE KWONDO

history *and* philosophy

Tae kwondo is derived from several martial arts, with the main influence being tae-kyon – Korean kick fighting. *Tae* means "to kick" or "smash with the feet"; *kwon* means "to intercept" or "strike with the hands"; and *do* means "the way of the art". Thus, the foundation of the art is the use of the hands and feet to overcome an attacker swiftly.

Tae kwondo was originally developed in Korea in the 1950s, when a group of leading martial arts experts came together to unify their respective disciplines under a single fighting system. The inauguration took place in South

Korea on 11 April, 1955, with Major-General Choi Hong Hi, a 9th-*dan* black belt, being credited as the founder. However, its roots stretch back nearly 2,000 years, when it was born from an art known as *hwarang do*, meaning "the way of the flowering manhood".

The *hwarang* were young noblemen, influenced by Confucian teachings, who formed a patriotic society during the unification of Korea, in the Silla dynasty, in about AD600. The Silla kingdom was the smallest of three within the Korean peninsula, and was constantly under attack from

The instructor demonstrates the flexibility and balance required by a kick to the head.

A scissor kick in tae kwondo, which is based upon ancient Korean martial arts.

its two stronger neighbours. It was these constant invasions that led the Silla nobility to develop a fighting system to protect their kingdom.

Towards the end of the 10th century, following the unification of Korea, learning tae kwondo became compulsory for all young men. However, in about the 16th century the military traditions of the country fell out of general favour and the practice of tae kwondo was kept alive only by Buddhist monks. Following the Japanese occupation in 1909, the suppression of any form of martial art only served to further its decline. The few remaining dedicated practitioners emigrated to China and Japan and, thus, the art survived.

Following liberation in 1945, many Korean exiles returned to their homeland and reintroduced an improved version of tae kwondo. The Korean government, as part of its campaign to reassert national identity following years of Japanese occupation, supported the practice of tae kwondo by officially sponsoring it. This led to a more formal approach to the teaching and grading of the discipline.

Tae kwondo spread worldwide from Korea in the 1960s, and the first World Tae Kwondo Championship took place in Seoul, South Korea, in 1973. Since 1988, tae kwondo has been listed as an Olympic sport.

Competition fighting

Competition fighting in tae kwondo is purely optional. For those who participate, competitions are split into three sections: sparring, patterns and destruction.

Sparring involves two practitioners practising fighting techniques to develop their timing, focus and speed. It is performed in a controlled environment so that no unnecessary injuries occur. In competition, the aim is to score points through the delivery of correct techniques to target areas.

Patterns are a set series of combination techniques performed in a sequential order against an imaginary opponent. This is similar to karate, which refers to patterns as *kata*, or kung fu, which uses set movements called "forms". One of the first patterns a practitioner learns is *chon ji tul* (the heaven and earth pattern).

Destruction refers to "breaking techniques", in which practitioners learn to break, for example, a piece of wood. The aim is to ensure that the power and skill of the technique are truly effective. It is also designed to focus the mind.

BENEFITS OF TAE KWONDO

Learning tae kwondo can have benefits in many different aspects of your everyday life. These include:

- Health and fitness
- Flexibility and stamina
- Confidence and well-being
- Self-awareness and assertiveness
- Comradeship
- Self-defence skills
- Stress reduction
- Positive attitude
- Strength of character
- Discipline of mind and body

clothing *and* equipment

Practitioners in tae kwondo require a plain white heavy weight cotton suit. This consists of a plain V-neck white jacket and trousers with elasticated waist. Instructors of 1st-*dan* and above wear a slightly different suit (*dobuk*) which has black edging around the neck. Higher grades, 4th-*dan* and above, wear a black stripe down the side of the trousers. It is important to ensure that the suit (*gi*) is the right size for a smart appearance and to feel comfortable when practising various techniques. Protective clothing is worn on occasions when this is deemed necessary by both men and women – and usually when free fighting (sparring) is taking place or a public demonstration. Clothing should always be kept clean and tidy.

Clothing needs to be clean, comfortable and durable for the many kicking techniques practised.

BELT GRADINGS

10th-*kup*	White
9th-*kup*	White with yellow stripe
8th-*kup*	Yellow
7th-*kup*	Yellow with green stripe
6th-*kup*	Green
5th-*kup*	Green with blue stripe
4th-*kup*	Blue
3rd-*kup*	Blue with red stripe
2nd-*kup*	Red
1st-*kup*	Red with black stripe
1st-*dan* and upwards	Black

A gold tag denotes the level achieved for *dan* gradings.

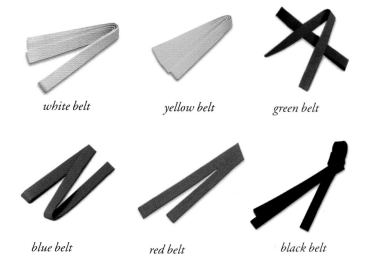

white belt   *yellow belt*   *green belt*

blue belt   *red belt*   *black belt*

Etiquette

There is only one bow performed in tae kwondo as part of etiquette and discipline. Practitioners perform a bow (*kyong ye*) upon entering the training area (*dojang*) as a sign of respect to the training environment. This bow is performed also to the instructor and students as a sign of respect prior to instruction or training.

❶ ◁ Stand in a relaxed position, with your feet a shoulder-width apart, and your hands held behind your back.

❷ ◁ Bring your open hands to the sides of your body and bring your feet together, with your heels touching and your toes slightly apart.

❸ ▷ Bow, lowering your body approximately 30 degrees, with your eyes looking forwards.

Exercise | Warm-up

Tae kwondo specializes in leg techniques and the following exercises assist in gently stretching all the muscles and sinews required before practice. By correct stretching and toning of the whole body, we work towards minimizing any injury. The following depicts a selection of exercises to be found in tae kwondo, showing the flexibility which can be achieved.

WARM-UP 1 – *This exercise will stretch your legs, hamstrings and inner thighs.*

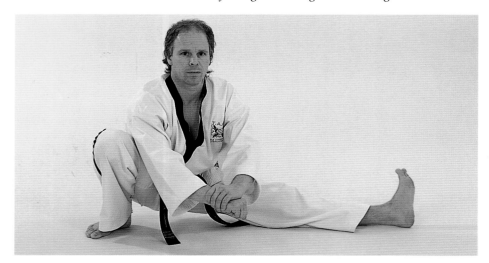

◁ Lower your body into a squatting position and push your left leg out to the side so that it is flat to the floor and with your toes pointing upwards. Clasp your hands in front of your body and try to maintain an upright posture. Repeat this exercise on the opposite side. This is not an easy exercise to perform in the early stages, so do not worry if you are unable to lower your leg as depicted. As long as your leg is kept straight, regular practice will enable you to become very supple.

WARM-UP 2 – *This is a hip-joint exercise.*

▷ While sitting on the floor, place your left leg across your right thigh. Place your right arm across your left knee and pull your left leg backwards. Ensure that your right heel is tucked well back towards your right thigh. Look in the opposite direction from your knee when levering your left leg backwards to cause a twisting action on your body. Repeat on the opposite side.

WARM-UP 3 – *Designed to stretch your legs and body generally, this exercise is particularly beneficial for your lower back and the backs of your legs.*

◁ Sit on the floor and pull your right heel into your groin area. Keep your left leg straight with your foot and toes pulled back. Lean forwards from the waist and grab your left foot with both hands. Try, if possible, to lower your head on to your knee, keeping your leg straight and flat to the floor. This may not be possible in the early stages but, with practice, you will eventually be able to achieve this position quite comfortably.

WARM-UP 4 — *This exercise is particularly useful for stretching your hamstrings, and increasing mobility of the hips, calf muscles and knee joints. Repeat this exercise to the right side. Again, the degree of flexibility may vary depending upon experience.*

❶ ◁ Sit on the floor and push your legs apart as far as you comfortably can. Take hold of your left ankle or foot with both hands and pull your body downwards towards your left knee. Try to touch your knee with your forehead. Bear in mind that it takes time for your muscles to become sufficiently supple to allow you to perform this exercise to its full extent. Hold this position for only a few seconds and repeat on the opposite side.

❷ ◁ With your legs still apart, take hold of both ankles. Lower your body as far as you can, with the aim of trying to touch the floor with your forehead. Hold this position for a few seconds only and do not worry if your head does not touch the floor, it is the actual lowering movement which stretches the relevant muscles and this must be built up gradually. Again, this is a very difficult exercise to perform if you are not extremely supple. Be patient – it may take months before you can fully achieve this movement.

WARM-UP 5 — *An important part of the warm-up routine is preparation for kicking.*

❶ ◁ With your partner turned away from you, place both of your hands on his shoulders for support. Swing your right leg sideways and as high as you can and repeat the exercise several times to loosen your thighs. Repeat the exercise with your left leg. Try to keep your leg as straight as possible.

❷ ▷ A similar exercise is to swing your leg, first forwards and then to the rear, while resting the side of your face on the top of your partner's back. Repeat this exercise several times with your right leg and then your left.

WARM-UP 6 — *Advanced exercise utilizing a partner to assist in stretching the inner thighs.*

> **CAUTION**
> This exercise must be performed only under professional supervision. Both partners must be well experienced and of similar weight and build.

◁ Sit on the floor and draw your feet in towards your groin, so that your knees are splayed out. Your partner, from the rear, gently places both hands on your shoulders for balance. He then carefully places his feet on your knees but does not, under any circumstances, bear down with all his weight on your knees. It is important that your partner maintains good balance and control as he gently pushes down on your knees. It is not the intention initially to bring your knees flat to the floor, as this could cause severe discomfort or even injury, but over a period of time you will come closer and closer to achieving this.

Technique | Basics

There are a variety of basic techniques in tae kwondo, of which the following demonstrates two blocks and strikes. These are designed to develop the skills required in tae kwondo and beginners need to practise slowly in the early stages. Speed will come in time, with practice.

BASIC TECHNIQUE 1 – *Lower parry block and spear hand strike to the chest.*

1 △ Face your partner in a formal stance with your right foot forward. Make sure that you have a good bend on your front knee and that your back leg is straight. Your partner adopts a left forwards stance, with his left leg forwards and right rear leg straight. Your partner then aims a punch at you with his left hand as he moves in towards you. Your response is a right-arm downwards palm block to prevent contact while you bring your left hand back, fingers straight and palm uppermost, in preparation to strike.

2 △ Strike your partner with your spear hand, aiming for your partner's solar plexus. Your thumbs should be tucked in and your fingers straight and locked together. Ensure that your right hand is under your left elbow to give support to the striking technique.

BASIC TECHNIQUE 2 – *Middle body block and ridge hand strike to temple.*

1 △ Remaining in the same stance, aim a punch towards your partner's solar plexus with your right fist. Your partner brings his left hand around in a semi-circle to deflect your attack.

2 △ Your partner then moves through to strike with the ridge of his right open hand to the side of your neck.

Technique | Self-defence for women

The following tae kwondo techniques are demonstrated as useful self-defence skills for women, although they are also applicable to men and children. The emphasis here is to develop confidence to handle an aggressive situation successfully by practising a strong stance, good posture and effective delivery of a technique.

SELF-DEFENCE 1 – *Elbow defence.*

CAUTION
When training with a partner, never apply a full-contact technique. Ensure that you aim your strike with care. It is only experienced practitioners who will have the ability to execute techniques that almost make contact.

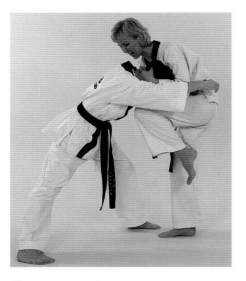

❶ △ Face your partner. As she strikes at your solar plexus with a left fist, step back with your left leg into a back stance, with about 70 per cent of your body weight on your rear leg, and deflect the attack with a circular open-hand knife-edge block. Ensure that your thumb is tucked in and your fingers firmly pushed together. Simultaneously, bring your left fist back to your hip in preparation to deflect or strike, whichever is required.

❷ △ Step through with your right leg and strike with your right elbow to your partner's mandible.

△ Here you can clearly see the elbow strike to the mandible. Note the scream (*kiai*). This is an exhalation of air that tenses the body and enhances the delivery of the strike.

SELF-DEFENCE 2 – *Knee defence.*

❶ △ Your opponent comes at you from the front and attempts to apply a stranglehold. Step back with your left leg, keeping a good bend on your front knee and with your rear leg straight. Keep both your hands in and then move them outwards in a double open-hand wedge block to deflect the strike.

❷ △ Take hold of the back of your partner's head with both your hands and pull her face forwards and towards your left knee.

❸ △ The conclusion to this technique is a fully executed knee strike to your partner's head. Remember, be careful when practising these exercises and aim to focus your techniques at least 4 in (10 cm) away from your partner's head.

Technique | Leg striking

The following is a selection of some of the superb leg-kicking techniques that are an integral part of tae kwondo. They are designed to strike the opponent from a variety of different angles and are particularly difficult for blocking. Tae kwondo uses a variety of sweeping, turning, spinning and jumping kicks as legs are a very powerful natural weapon.

TURNING KICK – *Using the ball of the foot to strike with an outwards, inwards kicking motion.*

TWISTING KICK – *Using the ball of the foot to strike with an inwards, outwards kicking motion.*

◁ This is fundamentally a spinning kick to catch your opponent on the move. This technique requires a lot of practice to perfect into a proficient leg-striking technique. Note the unusual angle of the kick and the alignment of the body.

❶ △ With your left foot firmly planted on the floor, lift your right knee as high as you can to the side. Ensure that your fists are in a front guard position. Look directly at your opponent.

❷ △ Bring your right leg around to the front in a circular movement as you fully extend it into a kick. The aim is to strike your opponent with the ball of the foot.

JUMPING SIDE KICK – *Using the side of the foot when elevated in order to strike.*

DOWNWARD KICK, OR AXE KICK – *Using the heel to deliver a strong kick from a high raised position.*

◁ The aim of the axe kick is to raise your leg as high as possible, and then bring the heel down hard enough to break an opponent's collar bone.

△ This is often viewed as one of the most spectacular of leg-striking techniques. Practitioners aim to reach great heights through constant training. A skilled practitioner, utilizing the jumping-side kick, can easily strike the face of a tall opponent.

Technique | Children's leg-strikes

This selection of tae kwondo self-defence techniques is suitable for children to practise. Note that in all cases the kick falls well short of actual body contact to maintain safety. It is important that children only practise those techniques which will enhance their well-being and not hinder their physical development.

FRONT KICK – Ap chagi.

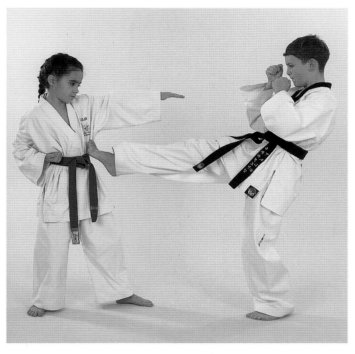

△ Demonstrating the front kick, striking with the ball of the foot to an aggressor's solar plexus.

SIDE KICK – Yap chagi.

△ A side kick to the solar plexus area is an effective deterrent, giving a child time to get to a place of safety.

BACK HEEL KICK – Dwit chagi.

△ Demonstrating a back heel strike to the solar plexus area.

TURNING KICK – Dollya chagi.

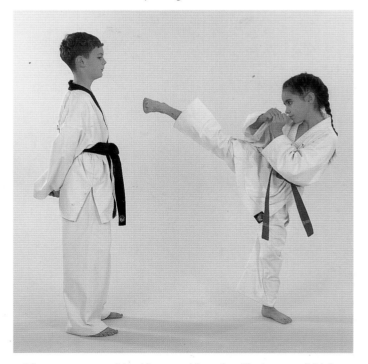

△ The momentum of the side turn adds to the effectiveness of this leg-striking technique, which uses the ball of the foot to make contact.

Women can enjoy tae kwondo training for a number of reasons, and whilst the following leg techniques are demonstrated by women, they are also utilized by both men and children. Women, in particular, will find that being able to deliver such skilled leg techniques can enhance their health, fitness, confidence and self-defence skills.

JUMPING TURNING KICK – *Catching the opponent off guard by jumping and striking the face area which is difficult to block.*

▷ Demonstrating a jumping turning kick, aiming for an opponent's throat or face.

BACK KICK – *Demonstrating flexibility of kicking techniques when striking to the rear.*

▽ A back kick to an opponent's solar plexus. This is known as a short range back kick where the leg is kept bent. There are similar techniques where the rear kick requires the leg to push back and become straight.

SIDE KICK FROM THE FLOOR – *A good self-defence technique.*

▷ Here is a demonstration of self-defence from what seems to be a vulnerable position. The side kick from the floor aims for an opponent's solar plexus, but could be equally effective if delivered to the groin, knee or shin.

ADVANCED
Technique | Kicking and breaking

The following demonstrates the skills that people, even those with major disabilities, can achieve. There are no barriers on the grounds of age, gender or ability, even though tae kwondo is viewed as a highly skilled leg-striking art. Dedication, discipline and perseverance are the qualities required, along with comradeship amongst all practitioners.

CRESCENT KICK

△ A very complicated move, involving a back twist, spin and jump kick. This movement is achieved by swinging the leg in a crescent motion towards the target area.

SIDE KICK

△ This is a side kick to the head. Note the introduction of protective equipment. In tae kwondo practitioners are required to wear hand mitts, shin guards, feet protectors, gum shields (mouth guards), head guards and groin protection (athletic cup), along with any other necessary equipment, when performing sparring.

BACK-HOOK TECHNIQUE

△ Note the good posture and balance involved in this back-hook technique. The practitioner receiving the strike has complete confidence that the strike will be well focused and that no contact will be made.

TURNING KICK

△ Demonstrating a turning kick to the back of an opponent's head. Again, note the good posture and body guard and how the top of the foot is being used to deliver the strike. In a street-defence situation the instep of the foot could be used to strike. The ball of the foot can also be used when performing breaking techniques.

BREAKING TECHNIQUE

Caution: Do not practise this technique without strict professional supervision. Breaking techniques are for demonstration purposes only and they show the powerful leg techniques of the art. They can take years to perfect.

△ The ball of the foot being used to perform a breaking technique.

TAI CHI CHUAN

Tai chi chuan combines the *yin* and *yang* approach of serene movements for health and well-being with a strong fighting system of self-defence. It is an excellent discipline for people of all ages and abilities, including children as young as five years of age. Older people also benefit fron tai chi chuan, such as the 81-year-old Chinese Grand Master Jiang Hao Quan, who is convinced that his youthful appearance, healthy mind and body are all due to his tai chi chuan training.

太極拳

TAI CHI CHUAN

history *and* philosophy

The initial aim of tai chi chuan is to teach the practitioner to relax. "Relax" in this sense does not mean to flop loosely around, but rather to use the body as efficiently as possible, with no muscular tension. The foremost requirement is good posture with relaxed shoulders, an upright back and firmly rooted stance. Tai chi chuan incorporates chi kung exercises, which encourage deep breathing, improved blood circulation and greater efficiency of the body's systems. On a mental level, the quiet concentration required for tai chi chuan brings a serene state of mind, in which the everyday stresses of life can be placed in their proper perspective. This

leads to a more tolerant, even state of mind, and a calm mind is able to respond more quickly and effectively to challenges in any situation.

At this level, the art is accessible to anyone – age, health or infirmity are not barriers to reaping some of the rewards that tai chi chuan has to offer. However, to reach the higher levels it is necessary to study the art in its wider context. Practising the martial aspects of tai chi chuan involves more complex forms of chi kung, body strengthening, two-person practice and various supplementary exercises. Such training is more demanding than basic-form practice, but it does bring greater benefits in terms of mental and physical health, as well as providing an excellent self-defence method. At the higher stages the theoretical aspects of the art also become more apparent.

As a martial art, tai chi chuan works on a number of levels, but the principal aim is to teach practitioners to relax and become fluid in their movements. This allows for smoother actions and quicker response times. The objective is for self-defence to become a reflexive action rather than a repetition of technique. There is a variety of sensitivity exercises which allow the practitioner to adapt instantly to an opponent and to react in the most appropriate manner. Incoming force will, typically, be diverted, however slightly, and the corresponding opening in the opponent's defence exploited. The level of response can range from applying

Chang San Feng, the legendary founder of tai chi chuan.

The tranquillity of early morning practice.

Practice in public places is not uncommon.

locks and holds, to immobilizing an opponent, through to highly damaging strikes against nerve centres and acupuncture points (*dim mak*).

The origins

Tai chi chuan is usually translated into English as "the supreme ultimate fist". The term *tai chi* refers to the *yin-yang* symbol prevalent in Chinese culture, more commonly known as the "hard" and "soft" sign – the two opposites coming together. The term *chuan* refers to a boxing method – boxing in this context means a method of empty-hand combat, rather than a sporting contest. Thus, as the name suggests, tai chi chuan is a self-defence method, one that is based on the Chinese Taoist philosophy of life.

Tai chi chuan is also referred to as internal kung fu. The reference to "internal" here refers to the general rule that tai chi emphasizes the development of the internal aspects of the body – breathing, flexibility and the mind – as opposed to external tension or muscular strength.

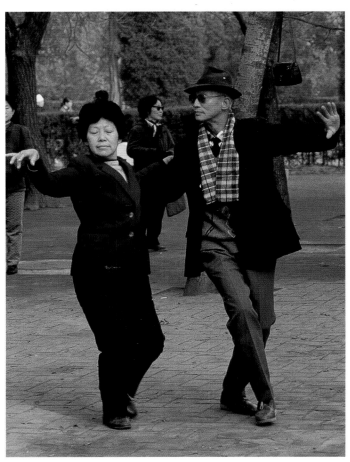

The roots of tai chi chuan are enshrouded in myth, and all but lost in legend, but the most popular theory refers to the art being originated by Chang San Feng, who was born in 1247. Chang studied at the famous Shaolin temple and mastered its system of martial arts. He then travelled to Wutang Mountain, a region populated by Taoist hermits where, as the legend goes, Chang watched as a stork and a snake fought. Fascinated by the fluidity of their movements and their ability both to evade and attack simultaneously, Chang adapted his system to incorporate the movements he had witnessed. It is also said that Chang had developed a high degree of skill in striking the body's acupuncture points, which he also incorporated into his art, though heavily disguised.

Yang Lu Chan (1799–1872), the undefeated founder of the Yang Family tai chi chuan.

Flowing and serene movement in group practice.

This art was passed down in great secrecy for many generations, eventually reaching the Wang family. The Wang family passed it on to the Chen family, who absorbed it into their own system, known as *pao chuan* (meaning "cannon fist"). The art at this stage was not called tai chi chuan: that name came to be applied only many years later. The Chens were held in high regard for their martial prowess and this attracted Yang Lu Chan (1799-1872) to the Chen village. The art was still being taught in great secrecy but, through his dedication, Yang was able to learn from the head of the style, Chen Chan Hsing. Then, after a short period of studying with the Wang family, Yang travelled to the imperial capital of Peking.

Once in Peking, Yang met many challengers from other styles of martial art, but remained undefeated, earning the nickname "Invincible Yang". Due to his reputation, Yang was ordered to teach the imperial family and the Manchu imperial bodyguard. It was impossible to ignore such a decree, yet Yang taught just a part of the art to the unpopular Manchu, retaining the knowledge of the complete system only for close family and trusted students.

Tai chi chuan's popularity began to spread among the nobility of the day and Yang's sons, both of whom were formidable fighters, continued this process, although the art was to some extent modified to suit the less rigorous lifestyles of the rich.

Transitionary process

It was during the 1920s that tai chi chuan really began to spread to different parts of the country. China at that time was in turmoil, with the population sick and ailing. The health benefits of the art became recognized and the once-secret art of the Chen family became a national exercise. You should note, however, that the art in its more popular form contains only part of the training of the traditional family styles, which, even today, are taught only to close students in order to maintain their secrecy and discretion. The main family styles – Chen, Yang, Hao and Wu – form the basis for many variations of style and form. Since the 1960s the art, in many guises, has spread to the West, making it a truly global phenomenon and the most widely practised martial art in the world.

Conclusion

Power training consists of chi kung to develop internal strength, as well as methods to strengthen the tendons and ligaments. The ability to issue power (*fa jing*) from close range is a primary feature of tai chi chuan. This involves incorporating the whole body into one unit behind an attack. Tai chi chuan includes punches, kicks, locks, open-hand techniques and throws in its repertoire, as well as traditional Chinese weapons: sword, broadsword, staff and spear.

Today, while traditional practitioners of tai chi chuan are still in evidence, the majority practise the art in order to both maintain and improve their health and to provide an increasingly necessary antidote to the stresses and strains of modern-day life.

BENEFITS OF TAI CHI CHUAN

- Enhances the ability of the practitioner to maintain an inner calm
- Enhances motivation and performance in all areas of life, such as work, social and home life
- Increases flexibility of muscles and movement of the body
- Increases quality of life through the "inner-calmness" approach to difficult situations
- Works towards a healthy mind and body, which can slow down the ageing process
- Reduces stress by increased awareness of relaxation skills

- Reduces tension through the development of inner energy and calmness of mind
- Reduces the need for other stimulants, such as alcohol and drugs
- Develops deep concentration and mental focus
- Assists in calming breathing and heart and brain processes, which can help our emotional responses to situations
- Assists the flow of energy in the body, thereby reducing both mental and physical blockages
- Improves the sense of humour

clothing *and* equipment

The traditional clothing and equipment for tai chi chuan is much the same as that for other Chinese martial arts: a black mandarin suit, flat-bottomed shoes and the traditional weapons – staff, sword, broad sword and spear. Generally speaking, class students wear any suitable loose clothing. Traditional uniforms are usually reserved for special occasions and public demonstrations.

Other than this, there are also various types of equipment available, such as focus pads and kick bags used in self-defence training, or for various supplementary exercises, such as grip training and body conditioning. Protective clothing may be worn in some instances, such as for students who are just beginning to spar.

black mandarin jacket

black trousers

gim

broad sword

Standard clothing required for tai chi chuan.

Etiquette

Etiquette is important within most martial arts disciplines and is carried out as a sign of respect. For example, the following moves are performed at the beginning and the end of the training session, and before practising with a partner. This is a traditional tai chi chuan salute.

1 ◁ Stand in a relaxed position with your feet together and hands at your side. Keep your back straight and shoulders relaxed. Clear your mind and try to induce a feeling of inner calm.

2 △ Bring both hands up in front of your chest, making your right hand into a fist and keeping the left hand open, fingers together. Place your right hand in the palm of the left and keep your eyes looking forwards.

3 △ Make a 30-degree bow forwards, keeping your hands together and eyes looking forwards. This is done to show respect to the art and the ancestors of tai chi chuan and to your training partner during practice.

△ This profile view of the bow shows that the position of your arms is slightly extended forward. Move back into the upright position, ready to commence practice.

Exercise | Warm-up

Most exercises are performed gently and slowly to maintain a feeling of inner calm, while stretching and strengthening the body. The following demonstrates two warm-up exercises that are usually performed before practising the basic techniques. The purpose of the exercises is to promote suppleness and flexibility within the body.

WARM-UP 1 – *This exercise has been developed to help make the waist, hips and the lower back region more supple.*

❶ △ Stand upright with both hands cupped together and your thumbs touching. Bend your knees slightly to lower your posture. Both feet should be facing forwards. Place your left thumb on top of your right.

❷ △ Pull your left hand around the side of your body, with the right hand following in a flowing action. Make sure you keep your feet facing forwards as your hands move around your body in a circular motion.

❸ △ Draw your hands backwards in a circular motion, ensuring that your palms are always facing upwards, almost as if you are holding a small bowl, and then start to move your hands in front of your body.

❹ △ Continuing the flowing movement, bring your hands slowly and gently in front of the body. Breathe naturally throughout the exercise.

❺ ◁ Continue the flowing action, with your left hand moving across the body towards your head.

❻ ▷ Lean backwards from the waist, flexing your stomach muscles to strengthen and increase flexibility. From this position rotate the upper part of the body and then resume the original starting position.

△ This side view demonstrates the correct arch of the body.

WARM-UP 2 – *This exercise is designed to strengthen the arms and requires the controlled breathing described below.*

❶ △ Stand in the ready position with your feet a shoulder-width apart. Make both hands into fists by your hips, palms upwards. Make sure your posture is upright, knees are slightly bent and your feet are facing forwards.

❷ △ Slowly push your right fist forwards while exhaling. As you bring your fist back to the hip, inhale slowly. Perform this action slowly and with focus.

❸ △ Repeat the previous action, this time using your left fist, remembering to maintain the correct breathing pattern.

◁ This view shows the slightly bent knees and correct, upright posture.

❹ ▷ After performing this exercise several times, return both fists to your hips and bring your feet together.

Technique | Hook

A popular technique in tai chi chuan is known as *tan pien*, or the "hook" position. This technique has various applications, namely a strike using the back of the hand, wrist strike, striking with the fingers, blocking or breaking a gripping technique. This technique assists in opening the joints and stretching the tendons, to increase strength and flexibility.

1 ◁ Adopt a forwards stance with your left palm pushing forwards at chest height and your right arm extended to the rear with the hand in the hook position. Ensure that 70 per cent of your weight is on your front leg in preparation to move backwards.

▷ Note the angle of the hand and the fingertips touching in this detail of the hook position.

2 ▷ The rear foot turns outwards and the weight begins to move on to the back leg. This is a smooth and continuous motion. The left hand begins to drop as if blocking a striking technique.

3 ▷ This is the "snake creeps down" (*hsia shih*) position and it requires you to manoeuvre your body. Lower your posture by bending your back (right) leg so that your upper and lower leg form a 90-degree angle. Transfer about 70 per cent of your body weight on to your right leg. Keeping your back straight and eyes fixed on your imaginary opponent, slide your left arm down your left leg, palm uppermost and fingers outstretched.

Technique | Striking

In this exercise you need the assistance of a partner, who assumes the role of an aggressor and prepares to strike you. Here, tai chi chuan employs techniques in a continuous flow to successfully defend against an aggressive strike. The following demonstrates the method of moving in from medium distance to close range.

❶ △ While it could be argued that in a street situation an aggressor might not approach you in quite this fashion, it is important when learning and practising techniques that safety and basic movements are applied to learn distancing and timing.

❷ △ In this situation the aggressor has thrown a punch. Note how the defender adopts the hooking technique, described earlier in this chapter, and applies it as self-defence in a circular blocking and striking action. Fluidity and timing are very important for this technique to be applied successfully.

❸ △ The defender aims to strike the temple. Note how the fingers are pushed together, with the thumb locked, while the back of the hand makes contact on the temple region.

△ Demonstrating the correct hand position for accuracy on the pressure point.

❹ △ The defender moves through, with his left leg across the aggressor's right leg, and applies his right hand around the throat, while the left hand is placed on the side of the aggressor's body.

❺ ▷ An alternative finishing position is to move in as in step 3, but to place the right hand around the back of the aggressor's neck, aiming for the pressure point that will render the aggressor unconscious. Energy is then directed forwards and downwards to take the aggressor down to the floor.

Technique | Locking and striking

When practising with a partner, set techniques have been developed to enhance body distance and mental awareness. This technique enhances the skill of developing fluidity of movement from striking to grappling with an aggressor. While the movements look relaxing, the energy and skill applied make for an effective method of self-defence.

❶ ◁ As the defender in this exercise, you should adopt a more relaxed stance and alert demeanour than that shown by the aggressor, who has both fists forwards. Transfer about 70 per cent of your weight on to the back leg. Keep your left hand in the open position, palm forwards, in front of your chest. Your right hand covers the lower part of your body, ready to deflect a blow.

❷ △ Using a circular action with your arms, turn your hips forwards, towards the aggressor, to support a blocking action. Block the punch with the outside of your right forearm. This is known as the "ward-off", or "p'eng". Your left hand is positioned either to apply another defensive move or a strike.

❸ ▽ Strike with the heel of your left palm into the pressure point on the side of the aggressor's right ribs.

△ Showing the correct hand position to maintain close contact.

❹ △ Pull your right hand up and over the aggressor's striking fist. At the same time, bring your left hand along to the aggressor's elbow position. Then push down on the aggressor's pressure point at the elbow, while simultaneously pushing the aggressor's arm forwards and away from his face. This locks the wrist in position and restrains the aggressor. At this point, bring your right leg completely around the aggressor's right leg, in preparation to apply a throwing technique.

TAI CHI CHUAN · TECHNIQUE · TECHNIQUE

Technique | Escape – rear defence

Many people fear being grabbed from the rear, especially around the throat. The following movement describes one of the many defences that can be applied to release such an attack, followed by an effective restraint. This demonstrates the effective self-defence element in tai chi chuan.

1 △ In this scenario, an attacker has grabbed you around the throat with his left arm, taking hold of your right wrist with his right hand.

2 △ Bring your free left hand up and take hold of the aggressor's left hand at your throat, aiming for the pressure point that is situated between the thumb and the forefinger. At the same time, step back with your right foot and bend forwards to start to unbalance the aggressor.

△ Make sure that you take a firm grip of the aggressor's hand as you start to pull the hand and arm away from your throat. Step backwards also, to prepare for the full disengagement.

3 △ Pull your body forwards in a downwards motion, at the same time pulling your left hand down and your right arm across your body. This pulls the opponent further off balance. Note that your rear leg is straight and your front leg is bent at 90 degrees.

4 △ With the aggressor now unbalanced, use your elbow to aim a blow at his solar plexus. Now bring your right leg behind the aggressor's left leg in preparation to perform an arm restrain. Push his left arm over your head into a locking position, maintaining a low posture by ensuring a good bend on your left leg and keeping your back leg straight.

5 △ Push the aggressor's left arm down, making sure that the arm is straight by securely holding the wrist with your left hand and placing your right hand in an upwards fist position, against the aggressor's arm.

6 ▽ Continue to apply pressure as you push the aggressor to the floor.

Technique | Pushing hands

There are various types of sensitivity training, and the most well-known is pushing hands (*toi sau*). The following is just one example of a basic technique of the pushing hands method for which tai chi chuan is famous. *Toi sau* develops the practitioner's awareness, sensitivity, skills and anticipation of an opponent's movement.

1 ◁ As you can see, the age, height and gender of the partners in this exercise are irrelevant. Here, the woman (partner 1) places her right hand, palm inwards, in the defensive "ward-off" position against the man's (partner 2) open-hand, forwards position.

2 ▷ Partner 2 pushes partner 1's hand towards her chest area. She deflects the push by turning and performing a circular action.

3 △ Partner 1 continues the circular action in a flowing motion, pushing forwards. It is very much like a circular, flowing action, twisting the side of the hand and the palm around. Partner 1 is now pushing towards partner 2's chest in a reversal of the original stance.

4 ▷ Partner 2 now allows the circular action to go across his partner's body and towards the right side, preparing to push back into the centre as a prelude to repeating the whole exercise.

Tai chi chuan utilizes a variety of weapons, including straight sword, staff and broad sword/sabre. Below are a sample of some of the moves taken from various *kata*, or sequences of set moves, demonstrating the use of the swords in both defensive and striking actions.

▷ This balanced stance is known as "lifting the leg to pierce" and it is used in a stabbing action.

△ "Drift with the current." This is a slicing action to the lower leg.

▽ The broad sword is kept out of view in preparation to strike. This technique is known as "conceal the sabre to kick".

△ This technique is known as the "big dipper" and is used when the practitioner is blocking with the straight sword and preparing to strike with the left leg.

△ "Turning the sword/sabre to pierce."

KENDO

On first impressions, kendo appears to be very physical and aggressive, with the dynamics of a fast-striking action and high-pitched screams. Yet it is an art that places great emphasis on the development of a high level of skill in concentration, timing, awareness, physical agility, footwork, body movement and inherent respect. Kendo was derived from the ancient art of Japanese *samurai* swordsmanship. Armour is worn for protection, and a sword made of four sections of bamboo is bound together to make what is known as a *shinai*.

KENDO

history *and* philosophy

Kenjutsu is the earliest martial art, dating back to before 1590, followed by kendo, which had more intellectual and philosophical characteristics. Kenjutsu became modern kendo, which has developed a sport-orientated nature that still embodies many of the traditional values.

It is believed that the origins of kenjutsu are located in the classical Chinese era, which dates back more than 2,000 years. However, while kendo is very much a modern art that has been influenced by kenjutsu, its roots can be traced back as far back as AD 789 through the history of the art of the sword which is linked inextricably to the history of ancient Japan. It was at this time that *Komutachi*, the sword exercise, was introduced as an instruction for the sons of the *kuge* (noblemen) in the city of Nara, then the capital of Japan.

Today's kendo very much relates to the changes in swordsmanship that came about in the early Tokugawa period of around 1600–1750. At this time, Japan embarked on an increasing period of stability, and the change from kenjutsu to kendo took place. It was not until the end of the 18th century, however, that the *shinai* (bamboo stick) became commonly used in basic practice. *Kendoka* (kendo students) would also work with the *bokken* (a wooden replica of a sword) and the *katana* (a practice sword).

Kendo should not be seen as a sport but as a lifetime's study.

It is interesting to note that, for the greatest part of Japanese history, kendo and/or kenjutsu were practised almost exclusively by the *bushi*, known more commonly today as the *samurai*. Today, people of all walks of life, gender, abilities and cultures can be found practising the art of kendo. No longer is it just confined to the boundary of

Kendo was derived from the art of Japanese samurai *swordsmanship.*

Japan, as it opens its doors to many other countries worldwide. It can also be said that kendo, like other martial arts, is a unifying activity, creating a sense of harmony through its competitive element. This was witnessed in March 1997 when the Heian shrine in Kyoto opened its doors to representatives from around the world to demonstrate the art of iaido, another martial art. At the same time, teams from many different countries took part in the tenth World Kendo Competition.

As with iaido, the philosophy of kendo is challenging. In many ways, it is viewed as contradictory by those who do not appreciate the importance of abandoning their own desires. This is not easy in a competitive world, with its increasingly materialist attitude, but as Musashi Miyamoto, one of Japan's most famous swordsmen (1584–1645), once said: "to win the battle is to be prepared to die."

This is very much the philosophy of the *kendoka*. Practitioners who enter into a fight, primarily concerned with not being hit, will find that their adversaries will more easily score points or win the battle. In kendo, the strike is viewed as a by-product of what has come before and what is

THE CONCEPT OF KENDO

The following is an extract from the All Japan Kendo Federation, highlighting the true concept of kendo and the purpose of practising this art:

- To mould the mind and body
- To cultivate a vigorous spirit

Through correct and rigid training:
- To strive for the improvement in the art of kendo
- To hold in esteem human courtesy and honour
- To associate with others with sincerity
- To pursue forever the cultivation of oneself

Thus, you will be able:
- To love your country and society
- To contribute to the development of culture
- To promote peace and prosperity among all peoples

about to follow, and there is a strong emphasis placed on initiative and taking control (*seme*). This plays an important part in kendo development, along with a constant sense of readiness and alertness (*zanshin*).

The aim of kendo is for *kendoka* to react intuitively, with fluency and elegance. Speed and body movement are of the utmost importance in the delivery of a skilful technique. Yet the aim is not to be the first one to score a point or to win in the kendo practice, but to work together, striving towards good technique, giving and taking along the way. Only in competition should this philosophical aim be different.

On first learning kendo, or any other martial art, it is very important to tread slowly. It is very easy when people wear armour to suddenly feel they can dive in regardless, without appreciating the need for continual practice to develop the skills to a standard acceptable in the art. It is important not only to demonstrate proficiency in the art but to ensure safe practice, both for yourself and your partner.

Kendo places great emphasis on moral values, discipline and self-control. Try to think of kendo not as a sport that you might participate in for a few years, but as a lifetime's study. Mental and physical control are of the utmost importance, since the balance of the two leads to harmony, not only in the art itself, but in your general well-being. It is for this reason that there are four deep-rooted mental hurdles that *kendoka* must overcome: fear, doubt, surprise and confusion. Collectively, these are known as "the four poisons of kendo".

Competition (*shiai*)

When experienced practitioners come together, especially in competition (*shiai*), the atmosphere can be very exciting. Competition is a vital part of kendo, since it provides an opportunity for practitioners to try out, under conditions of pressure and stress, the various techniques. The judges look for good posture, composure and the ability to deliver a strike effectively with all the skill and mental confidence that is required to show a good *kendoka*.

In an effort to avoid kendo competition becoming a violent, attacking activity (sometimes referred to as "bash and dash") based solely on winning, it is important that *kendoka*, especially beginners, develop the mental confidence to remain calm (*shiai geiko*). *Kendoka* strive to remain calm, alert and decisive, and to accept defeat as a guide to developing their technique and skill for the future. A kendo *shiai* usually lasts for five minutes, and the winner is the first to score two points, or a single point if the time limit elapses first. There are three court referees and a senior referee off court. There is also a timekeeper to ensure that the competitors are within the allocated match period. The rules of the competition are always strictly adhered to.

More than 5,000 Japanese boys and girls during the All Japan Children's Military Arts Summer Training Meeting held in Tokyo.

Kendoka *demonstrating the dynamics of the fast cutting action and fighting spirit.*

Scoring in kendo

During the *shiai* there are many opportunities for *kendoka* to learn and refine their skills. For example, there are differences between *shiai* (contests) and *dojo jigeiko* (free practice). This is perhaps best demonstrated in the example of opponents fighting within the parameters of the rules set by the leading organizations. This will result in a winner and a loser and, in comparison to Olympic fencing, where a point is scored simply by making contact with the target, in kendo several elements are required in order for the essential winning point to be scored. These include:

• Creating an opportunity to attack a vulnerable point on the body.

• The accuracy and skill of the strike itself, which must be delivered with the correct spirit – sword and body working together as one.

A very important part of kendo training is *zanshin*, which translates as "good awareness" – that is, of the opponent and the continuing element of battle. It is the ability to take in the environment, being sensitive to any threat or other factors that could lead to injury, even death. *Zanshin* enables *kendoka* to attain a heightened ability and awareness, and thus to react instantaneously to minimize risk.

BENEFITS OF KENDO

The benefits derived from learning kendo affect many aspects of your everyday life. These include:

• **Speed and agility**
• **General fitness**
• **Self-discipline and a positive attitude**
• **Precision and timing**
• **Self-confidence**
• **Self-control and well-being**
• **Comradeship**
• **Inner peace and calm**

clothing *and* equipment

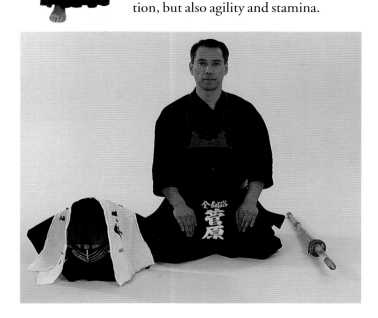

Kendo developed and evolved from actual battlefield conditions and therefore the utilization of armour became essential and intrinsic to the practitioners of this art. As a full contact art, the relevant parts of the body must be well protected. For example, the head guard (*men*) is of extremely durable quality and can withstand the constant strikes made with the *shinai*. There is a set procedure for putting the armour on and great pride is taken to ensure that this is well-maintained, clean and correctly laid out before every training session. Practitioners practise sword exercises prior to any kendo training session, to maintain not only the tradition, but also agility and stamina.

*Practitioner (*kendoka*) sitting (*seiza*) in preparation to place the head armour (*men*), gloves (*kote*) and* shinai *in the correct position, before commencement of practice.*

The kendoka *prepared, fully armoured, bowing (*rei*) to either the dojo, instructor or opponent. Note the* shinai *is in a lowered and relaxed position.*

do *(body protection for chest and side)*

men *(helmet to protect the head, face and neck)*

kote *(gloves for wrist and hand protection)*

kote

tare *(lower body protection)*

tenugui *(head cloth worn under the* men*)*

bokken *with* tsuba

suburi bokken

shinai

SAFE PRACTICE AND *DOJO* ETIQUETTE

- It is important that you do not touch a practitioner's armour or *shinai* (bamboo sword), *bokken* (wooden sword) or sword, without that person's permission. It is very important that you not only respect your own clothing and equipment, but also that of fellow practitioners.
- Always treat your *shinai* with respect. Never lean on it when being given instruction or discard it in the *dojo* without respect. Treat your *shinai* as a sword, since this is what it truly represents.
- Never step over a fellow practitioner's *shinai* or armour when it is laid out, whether it is in the *dojo* ready for practice or at the side of the *dojo* in preparation.
- If your armour comes loose, or any of your clothing slips and you need to retie it, move to the side of the *dojo* opposite the *kamiza* (known as the *shimoza*). Go into a kneeling posture (*seiza*) and then readjust your clothing and armour. Never, under any circumstance, adjust, retie or reposition your armour or clothing while standing as this is viewed as disrespectful and puts you at risk of attack in a real battle situation.

Etiquette

Dojo etiquette is very important in kendo. It is aimed at teaching *kendoka* (practitioners) respect for the *dojo* (training environment), their opponents and themselves. While *dojo* etiquette may vary slightly from one kendo club to another, around the world, the following is considered as standard.

SAFETY IN THE *DOJO*

- As you enter the *dojo* perform a bow (*rei*) to the *kamiza* – the area designated as the shrine or that is considered to be the point at which respect is given.
- You should always acknowledge the instructor (*sensei*) with a bow, or some other form that is considered appropriate, as he or she enters the *dojo* or gives you instruction or advice.
- Always be punctual and try to arrive early for training. This demonstrates discipline, respect and dedication.
- Remove your shoes when entering the *dojo*. Not only does this show respect for your training area, it is also hygienic. The Japanese don't usually wear outdoor footwear inside.
- Never drink, smoke or eat in the *dojo*.
- Ensure you are smartly dressed and that your clothing (*keikogi* and *hakama*) are well-pressed and clean. This demonstrates self-discipline and respect for the art.
- As a sign of respect and politeness, always pass behind any practitioner wearing armour. This shows respect and ensures safety in the *dojo*. If, however, you have to pass in front of an armoured practitioner who is seated, pause, make a slight *rei*, and extend your hand as you pass.
- If "*yame*" is called, you must immediately halt whatever you are doing. *Yame* is Japanese for "stop" and this rule applies to general practice, basics and competition.
- During all training, great emphasis is placed on manners (*reigi*) and respect. As with any sport or discipline, there is always a potential for injury, and so it is very important that you maintain self-control and a respectful attitude towards everybody within the *dojo*.

THE BOW

1 ◁ Kneel down with your hands placed on your thighs. Keep your back straight and look to the front. This position is called *seiza*. Place your armour neatly at your right side with the guard (*tsuba*) on the sword handle level with your left knee. You should keep a relaxed yet assertive posture.

2 ◁ As you lower your body forwards, place the palm of your left hand, then right hand, flat on the floor, making a diamond shape, with your forefingers and thumbs touching. Keep your elbows tucked in and perform the bow (*rei*) as a sign of respect to the *dojo*, instructor and the practice that is about to commence. This *rei* is also performed to the spirit of kendo (*kamiza*), usually towards the practitioner's right side.

MEDITATION (*MOKUSO*)

This is a period of concentration, performed while kneeling, and is the position used at the beginning and end of both kendo and iaido training. It is important to rid yourself of any worries, concerns and distractions, and it is considered helpful to think of running water (*rishu*) as an aid. The nature of flowing water represents tranquillity – one drop may be meaningless in the context of many thousands, yet each drop in itself is part of an important element of nature.

◁ Bring your hands together, palms upward, in a cupped position. Close your eyes and breathe in slowly through your nose. Imagine the breath going up over your head and down into the pit of your stomach. Breathe out slowly through your mouth. The duration of this exercise varies, depending on your experience and your teacher's (*sensei's*) instruction.

Exercise | Warm-up

Practitioners perform a variety of warm-up exercises before putting on their armour. Great emphasis is placed on maintaining a high mental focus on the technical purity of the art. At the start of training, practitioners practise what is known as *keiko* (free practice). Further warm-up is performed, when wearing armour, at the start of training.

WARM-UP 1 – *Loosening your leg muscles and lower limbs.*

△ Step forwards with your right leg and place your hands on your hips. Keep your rear leg straight and apply a forwards and downwards pushing pressure. Change to your left leg forwards and repeat the exercise 2 to 3 times each side.

WARM-UP 2 – *Stretching the sides of your body for flexibility.*

△ Bring your right arm up and over your head and place your left hand on your hip. Keep your feet facing forwards as you stretch your arm over your head, as if trying to touch the floor with your fingers. Keep your body relaxed for maximum benefit. Change to your left arm and repeat the exercise 2 to 3 times each side.

WARM-UP 3 – *Stretching of legs, hips and upper body in order to increase mobility.*

△ Stand with your legs fairly wide apart and drop your hands so that your fingertips touch the floor. Repeat 3 to 4 times.

WARM-UP 4 – *An exercise to help stretch your body, with particular emphasis on leg muscles and controlled breathing.*

△ Keeping the same stance as in the previous exercise, take your right hand across to touch your left foot. Repeat on the opposite side, using your left hand to touch your right foot. Repeat the exercise 3 to 4 times each side.

Prior to any exercise using the *shinai*, perform a bow (*rei*) as a sign of respect to the art and your fellow practitioners. The *shinai* is made of four pieces of bamboo, which are bound together for lightness and strength. The following show the preparation needed prior to starting the basic cutting exercises and techniques.

SUBURI

Basic cutting exercises, known as *suburi*, are performed by the practitioner as part of basic practice, both prior to wearing armour and with full armour. The practice is also performed individually, in a group session or with a partner. The exercises are to develop technique, build strength, speed and stamina, with the additional benefit of developing focus, concentration and correct breathing. A shout, known as *kiai*, is made on the completion of each strike.

PREPARATION

❶ △ Stand in a formal position, with your feet facing forwards, back straight and chin up. Hold the *shinai* in a relaxed position in your left hand.

❷ △ Lower your body about 30 degrees to perform a bow (*rei*). This is performed to your instructor and also when opposite a partner before commencement of practice.

❸ △ Bring the *shinai* up to your left hip in preparation to move three paces forwards.

❹ △ Draw your *shinai* as you step forwards and go down into a squatting position (*sonkyo*). Keep your heels together with your feet facing outwards at a 45-degree angle. The *kendoka* (practitioner) on the left is demonstrating the angle of the draw, while the one on the right is in the *sonkyo* position.

❺ △ This is the standing position (*kamae*). The *kendoka* on the left is demonstrating the angle of the *shinai* in the forwards position. The *kendoka* on the right demonstrates the side view.

EXERCISE – *Following the preparation, various exercises can be performed using the* shinai.

❶ ◁ Place the *shinai* in the small of your back, just behind your hips, and rotate your hips and the *shinai* in a circular motion towards the right.

❷ ▷ Rotate the *shinai* in a circular motion towards your left side. Repeat several times.

Preparation | Wearing of armour

Before wearing the head guard (*men*), you must first put on a cotton cloth called a *tenugui*. This cloth serves three purposes: it soaks up perspiration to prevent it running into your eyes; it keeps your hair out of your face and eyes; and it acts as a cushion under the head guard. The *tenugui* usually displays *dojo* or country information.

FITTING THE HEAD GUARD (*MEN*)

1 △ Lay the *men* (head guard) to your right side on top of the *kote* (hand guard), making sure the *tenugui* is placed on top of your *men*. Your *shinai* must be placed to your left side with the *tsuba* in line with your left knee.

2 △ Lift the *tenugui* and stretch it out in front of your body.

3 △ Wrap the *tenugui* around your head. The *kendoka* on the left is demonstrating the position of the *tenugui* and ties, while the one on the right is showing how to tie the *tenugui* above the forehead.

4 ◁ The *tenugui* is now correctly tied in preparation for the *men*.

5 ▷ Secure the *men* by taking the cords or strings (*himo*) and wrapping them around your head. The *kendoka* on the left is showing the *himo* being pulled and wrapped around the *men*. The *kendoka* on the right, in profile, is showing the finishing position of the *himo*, neatly in place.

6 △ Next, the hand guards (*kote*) are put on – first the left and then the right hand. This ensures that the right hand is free for as long as possible, should it be necessary to defend against an attack. The *kendokas* are now ready to commence practice.

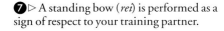

7 ▷ A standing bow (*rei*) is performed as a sign of respect to your training partner.

8 △ Lower your body into the squatting (*sonkyo*) position, balancing on the balls of your feet (heels touching) and with your knees at about 45 degrees. This is the start position of all practice in kendo, including basics, grading and competition. Hold the *shinai* out from the centre of your body, with your right hand gripping the handle (*tsuka*), above the left hand. Your partner squats opposite so that the tips of your *shinai* are just touching.

Technique

Basic competition (*shiai*)

△ A standing bow (*rei*) is performed as a sign of respect to your partner.

GOOD POSTURE

A vital part of being skilled in kendo is maintaining a well-balanced and upright posture. Whether you are moving forwards or backwards, correct body posture is an important part of delivering a strike that has the correct force and energy. Leaning to the side usually results in an ineffective strike leaving you vulnerable to attack.

STANCE

Your stance is an extremely important part of kendo practice. When standing normally, your feet should be a shoulder-width apart. Move forwards with your right foot, so that the heel is in line with the toes of your left foot. The heel of your left foot should be slightly raised – but no more than 1 in (2.5 cm), allowing you to move with agility and speed.

At the beginning of each basic competition (*shiai*) session, two contestants step into the contest area (*shiajo*) and bow to each other as a sign of respect. They then advance to the centre of the court, before drawing their shinai and sinking down into the squatting position (*sonkyo*). The main referee will shout "*hajime*" ("begin"), at which point the contestants stand and usually let out a shout, known as *kiai*, before initiating an attack. It is often thought that this relates to the philosophy of shouting as a way of generating fear within the opponent. Shouting is also thought to produce extra strength for the attack. The two contestants then try to score points by striking specific parts of the body: the head (*men*), the throat (*tsuki*), the sides of the body (*do*) or the wrist (*kote*). Even where a point is scored, contestants continue to maintain fighting spirit until the senior court judge yells "*yame*" (stop).

The contestants then reposition themselves at the centre of the court and the contest continues, until either one has scored the match point to win the *shiai*. At the end, both contestants lower themselves into the *sonkyo* position. As there is no *saya* (scabbard that protects the sword), the *shinai* is not sheathed but is placed in a natural position to the left side of the body (similar to wearing a sword). This is performed prior to and at the end of the competition. The contestants then walk away backwards, bow to each, turn and exit.

HAND POSITION

Your left hand should be as near to the base of the hilt of the handle of the *shinai* (bamboo sword) as possible, with your right hand just below the *tsuba* (the guard that divides the handle from the "blade"). A firm yet relaxed grip on the *shinai* is required – it is the third and fourth fingers of your hands that actually grasp the sword, while the rest of your hands, wrists, forearms and shoulders should be relaxed. Holding the *shinai* in a hard and aggressive way burns up unnecessary energy, leading to fatigue and an ineffective style. This hand position does not change throughout the practice, whether you are holding the *shinai* with or without gloves (*kote*). Once you have the correct grip, make sure that the hilt of the *shinai* is approximately one to two hand grips away from your lower abdomen. Don't rest the *shinai* against your body, since this is considered disrespectful.

Technique | Basic strikes

Striking techniques in kendo are mainly aimed at three areas of the body, namely the head (*men*), (centre, left and right) body (*do*) wrist (*kote*), with thrust or lunge (*tsuki*). These areas are well-protected with armour, but were vulnerable in the days of the *samurai*. Some striking terms have the same name as each area's protective equipment.

SHOMEN UCHI – MEN STRIKE
◁ *Shomen uchi* is a cut executed towards the top of the head (*men*).

△ Aim to strike the centre of the head with the end of the *shinai*.

▽ Counter-attack with *do waza* (body out). The aim is to cut the side of the body as the aggressor moves through to strike and presents a vulnerable position. This requires precision of timing and accuracy.

▽ Evading a *shomen uchi* strike to the top of the head and preparing to counter-attack.

KOTE

▽ This strike is known as cutting the wrist (*kote*), in which the *shinai* makes contact with the forearm anywhere between the wrist and about half way to the elbow. It is a strike coming from above, and cuts are permitted to the front of the arm if your opponent's *shinai* is in a low position, and to the left arm when it is raised, depending on whether your opponent is moving forwards or backwards.

CHUDAN TSUKI

△ A thrusting action to your opponent's throat. This is performed, especially in competition, to try and score a point. The partner is well-protected by a firm padded guard which covers the throat area.

DO

◁ This is a cut to the side of the body between the armpit and the hip bone. It can be performed from either side and is a diagonal cut from above.

△ Upon making contact with the armour, the practitioner making the strike will shout "*do*", as this is the part of the body they are striking.

Katata (THRUST)

▽ A single-handed thrust to your opponent's throat is known as *katata tsuki*. *Caution: this technique can be very dangerous, which is why kendo armour has protective padding, extending from the face grid to the breast bone. It is important that this part of the armour, in particular, is well-maintained, but even so, accidents have been known to happen, when the shinai has accidentally penetrated underneath the padding. Take great care that your armour is of good quality and is correctly fitted.*

△ In this close-up of the correct footwork, note the short stance, with the feet a shoulder-width apart, the weight on the balls of your feet and the rear heel slightly raised. This is the main stance adopted by all practitioners.

Men uchi

▽ The movement through to strike the head (*men*) is used in various exercises. For example, *keiko* (free practice), which is divided into various areas including *uchikomi keiko* and *keri kaishi*, during which students rapidly attack exposed target areas of their opponent with power and full concentration.

Tsuba zeriai

▽ *Tsuba zeriai* is the name given to this position, in which you and your opponent are very close together, with both *shinai* pushing against each other, looking for an opening from which to strike.

Jigeiko

When practitioners have been through the various exercises, they get the opportunity to put their training into practice against each other, in what is known as *jigeiko*. This is not a free-for-all session, but a time to develop their skill, timing and precision, and to fine-tune their techniques. This is a form of practice in kendo and is not specific to competition or grading.

IAIDO

Iaido is the art of drawing your sword and striking an armed opponent at lightning speed. It is the art of strategy, achieving precision in all aspects of mental and physical ability, including accurate footwork, balanced posture and critical timing. "Live" blades are razor-sharp and experienced practitioners are the only ones permitted to use them. The risk involved is thought worthwhile, because this is the only way to achieve the ultimate in awareness and concentration, and to bring mind and body together in total harmony.

IAIDO

history *and*
philosophy

Iaido derives from the ancient way of the *samurai* warrior (*bushi*), and the forerunner of the art we know today, *iai-jutsu*, was used in earnest on the battlefield, whereas iaido was designed to practise "the way of the sword".

Evidence suggests that the *bokken* used today in iaido has been used as a weapon since about AD 400. The *bokken* is a solid wooden stick with the same shape, weight and approximate length as a sword, and is usually made of red or white oak. *Bokken* technique was followed by the art of *tachikaki* (drawing the sword from its scabbard). The blade (*tachi* or *katana*), was long and straight and the Japanese warrior would carry it on his left side. A shorter blade was used for quick-draw techniques, known as *batto*.

The curved swords seen today are not the original Japanese swords. Indeed, they were flat, straight swords of primitive construction, used for simple strikes and thrusts. It was around AD 940, the middle of the Heian period, that the single-edged, slightly curved sword appeared, and the superb skill of the Japanese warrior developed. Until that time, single-handed swords were used in battle by mounted warriors. They were protected by heavy armour, using the right hand to draw and cut the enemy.

Sometime during the mid-16th century, battle strategy changed and mounted warriors replaced foot warriors who wore lighter armour and used techniques requiring both hands on the sword hilt.

Dominance of the *bushi*

In 1189, the *samurai bushi* of the Minamoto clan finally gained complete military and political dominance in Japan, a position they maintained for nearly 700 years, until 1868. In the early part of the 14th century, however, there was a

*Haruna Matsuo Sensei – 7th-*dan *iaido.*

Practitioners from all over the world practising iaido at the Heian Shrine, Japan.

decline in the military skills of the *bushi*, but this was rectified during the third Ashikaga Shogun Yoshimitsu period (1358–1508), when encouragement was given to proper training in such skills as archery, swordsmanship and the use of *naginata*, a curved blade spear.

The ability to draw the blade in a bold, fast and dynamic upward, sweeping movement, was intrinsic to the *bushi*. Nevertheless, this was not a standardized style of fighting, and it was during the early Heian period that much of Japanese culture was imported from China. It was not only the Chinese martial arts that captured the imagination and interest of the Japanese, it was also the study of Chinese philosophy, painting and poetry.

What is iaido?

Although iaido may be classed as a separate martial art, it is closely related and complementary to kendo. Kendo practice requires two people fencing each other armed with *shinai* (bamboo swords) and wearing armour, whereas iaido is practised on an individual basis wearing a *gi*, *juban*, *hakama* and *obi*. Practitioners use a real or an imitation sword, called an *iaito*. The aim of the exercise is to perform a set series of movements (*kata*), in which the sword is drawn, an imaginary opponent is cut, and then the sword is resheathed. The ultimate purpose of iaido, however, is to master the ability to overcome your enemy without the sword being drawn in the first place – in other words, to conquer your opponent "spiritually", with the sword still in the sheath, and so resolve problems without having to even resort to violence. There is one quote that explains this way of thinking: "Your mind is not disturbed by you being beaten up, but by you beating up others."

It has been said that many iaido moves passed down over the centuries were secret techniques related to Zen practice and enlightenment, as well as the secret physical techniques (*waza*). In the 15th century, a Zen master, Takuan, discussed with Yagyu Munenori, a sword master, the concept of the "unfettered mind". This was defined as a person who could remain calm in the face of adversity. They agreed on the word *fudoshin* to encapsulate this concept. The term came to describe any person who demonstrates clarity of mind and purpose, even in the most difficult situations.

There are various traditional styles of iaido still practised in Japan today, although many have been lost over the

The true spirit of martial arts is founded upon detail and correctness. Note the positioning of the feet, whereby further movement is easily effected.

centuries. Those that have survived have been passed down from generation to generation. These include muso jikiden ryu, muso shinden ryu and katori shinto ryu. These styles of iaido are based on the more traditional schools of swordsmanship, employing fast-drawing techniques.

It is widely believed that Hayashizaki Jinnosuke Shigenobu founded the school of iai jutsu (the precursor of iaido) in 1560. His sword techniques were perfected by Eishin in the 18th century, since which time the muso jikiden ryu style has developed, as well as the eishin ryu forms.

In 1968-69, a system known as seitei gata iaido was developed, in order to provide a basic system around which all the varied styles of iaido could be unified.

Competition (*taikai*)

Seitei gata iaido forms an important basis for gradings in iaido, no matter how senior or junior the grade. Many practitioners take part in competitions (*taikai*) throughout the year, and while there is an element of practitioners being able to demonstrate their own style, it is vitally important that

Assisting practitioners to develop their skills in iaido.

Two Japanese swordsmen illustrate the concept of zanshin *– total mental alertness and awareness.*

The meeting of blades.

they demonstrate the basic seitei gata iaido, so that the judges can truly evaluate their skills and techniques.

Taikai, in iaido, is performed by two practitioners running through their routines at the same time. Individual performance is judged by three referees who are looking and judging on a wide variety of technical, physical and mental attributes.

Many of the basic rules for the art of kendo also apply to iaido competition, with the addition of *kokorogamae*, which means "mental posture". *Kokorogamae* includes calmness, vision (*metsuke*), spirit, concentration, distance (between individuals) and timing. The Japanese expression of *shin gi tai-no-ichi* (meaning "heart, technique and body as one") sums up the aims of *kokorogamae* perfectly.

BENEFITS OF IAIDO

The benefits derived from iaido affect many aspects of your everyday life. These include:

• Speed and agility
• Fitness
• Self-discipline and a positive attitude
• Precision and timing
• Self-confidence
• Self-control and well-being
• Comradeship
• Inner peace and calm
• Harmony of mind and body

clothing *and* equipment

The colour of the *hakama* in iaido can range from white, black and blue, to pin stripe grey or other similar colours. The materials of the clothing also vary from the less expensive polyester and cotton fabric to silk. Practitioners usually wear a *zekken*, which is a chest patch embroidered with their name, *dojo* and nationality. Great pride is taken in appearance, ensuring that all clothing fits correctly. *Bokken* and swords should be well cared for, being cleaned and maintained regularly, after every practice. It is equally important to check *bokken* and swords prior to the commencement of practice, to ensure safety in the *dojo* environment.

Blue jacket The jackets are available in a variety of colours and material, black, white and blue are the most common colours worn.

Hakama A folded skirt, similar to culottes. There are five pleats at the front and one at the rear. Wearing a good-quality *hakama* is recommended, since it is extremely durable and will maintain its shape throughout practice.

Obi The long, wide, band that is wrapped around the body underneath the *hakama*.

Zori The sandals that are used mainly outside the *dojo*. They are designed to be slipped on to either bare feet or over the *tabi*. Never wear *zori* inside the *dojo* or when training as this is seen as both disrespectful and dangerous.

Tabi These are the formal footwear that are allowed in the *dojo*. They are usually of cotton material with a non-slip base.

Shinken The *shinken* is a "live" blade – razor-sharp and made in the traditional Japanese way, by folding the metal many times to obtain a blade that is light, yet incredibly strong. *Shinken* is expensive to buy, whether you purchase an original or a new blade.

CAUTION:
Live blades should never be used by beginners or inexperienced practitioners. Take the advice of your professional instructor about when the time is right for you to use a *shinken*. The use of a *shinken* is not required until you have attained the level of 6th-*dan* (*rokudan*). However, it is preferable to start using a *shinken* at 4th-*dan* (*yondan*) and above. It gives real meaning to the feel of iaido when a live blade is drawn.

Iaito The *iaito* is another type of practice sword used in iaido, which has a stainless-steel replica of a live blade (*shinken*).

Sageo The cord that is secured to the scabbard. The small wooden piece through which the *sageo* is fed is known as the *kurigata*.

Bokken Most people start iaido practice using either a *bokken* or an *iaito*. A *bokken* is a wooden replica sword, usually made of white or red oak, with the same shape (curvature) as a real sword and a plastic guard (*tsuba*). The disadvantage of using a *bokken* is that there is no *saya* (the sheath, or scabbard, that covers the blade). This means that the practitioner will not benefit from *saya* practice with the left hand, which is equally as important as the right hand in the art of iaido.

Tsuba The *tsuba* is the circular fitting which is placed between the handle (*tsuka*) and sword. On a *bokken* it is usually made of plastic and on a live blade can be a decorative piece of craftsmanship.

Zekken The embroidered patch with the practitioner's name, *dojo* and nationality written in Japanese.

Cleaning kit This comprises of *uchiko* powder, which is used to remove acidity and grime from the blade, caused through contact with the hand during practice. The powder ball is gently tapped on both sides of the blade, from base to tip, to cover it with powder.

Etiquette

Dojo etiquette is very important in iaido, not only as a sign of respect to the art, training area and fellow practitioners, but also to ensure everybody's safety. Etiquette is quite involved, as it follows Japanese tradition in placing great emphasis on the smallest detail. Using any weapon is dangerous if not handled with utmost respect.

1 △ Before walking on to the training area, hold your sword in your left hand with the blade (*hi*) facing upwards. When you arrive at your position for training, raise the sword to just below your waist (*taito*).

2 △ At this point, your sword hand is resting just above your left hip bone, with the sword angled slightly inwards at about 45 degrees.

△ Side view showing correct posture and angle of the sword.

3 △ Turn towards the *kamiza*, the area designated as the place of respect. This is usually, but not necessarily, towards the east of the *dojo*. You now pass the sword over to your right hand.

4 △ Turn the sword as you pass it from your left to your right hand, so that the edge of the blade is facing down towards the floor.

5 △ Bring the sword down and hold it at a 30-degree angle on the right of your body, with the edge of the blade facing downwards.

6 △ Bow to *kamiza*, ensuring minimum sword movement. This is a small bow only, so lower your upper body by no more than 15 degrees. Lower your eyes naturally as you bow. There is no need to keep looking forward, as you are bowing to the art, not an opponent.

7 △ Return to the upright position. Pass the sword back to your left hand. Make sure your thumb is looped around the cord (*sageo*).

8 △ Position the sword back on your left hip.

9 △ Lower your body into the kneeling position (*seiza*), keeping your eyes forward (*metsuke*) on your opponent. To prevent the *hakama* becoming entangled with your legs and feet, perform a V-shaped cutting action with the knife edge of your right hand, known as *hakama sabaki*.

10 △ Place your left knee down on the floor first, followed by your right knee.

11 △ Lower your body and settle on your heels. Rest the sword lightly on your left thigh and place your right hand near the top of your right thigh. Ideally, your hand should be just under the guard (*tsuka*), for ease of drawing the blade.

12 △ Pass the sword from your left hand to your right.

13 △ Holding the *sageo* with your left fingers, slide your left hand down the sword. Stop approximately 4 in (10 cm) before you reach the end of the scabbard (*saya*).

14 △ Hold the sword in front of your body as you pass the *sageo* underneath the sword with the fingers of your left hand.

15 △ Place the sword neatly on the floor, directly in front of you. Avoid making any unnecessary movements.

16 △ Next, place your left hand, then your right, on to your upper thighs.

17 △ Lower your body, placing your left hand on the floor, followed by your right, with thumbs and forefingers forming a diamond shape. With elbows tucked in, keep the back of your head in line with your spine as you perform the bow (*rei*).

18 ▷ Following the bow, revert to an upright kneeling posture. Take hold of the sword with both hands, with the palm of your right hand facing upwards and the left facing downwards. As you bring the sword back towards you, place your left thumb down the centre of your *hakama* to make an opening for the sword. Gently push the end of the scabbard (*saya*), known as the *kojiri*, through the ties of the hakama and *obi*, towards your left side, so that the sword sits comfortably, ready to commence practice.

19 △ Bring the *sageo* over the back of the *saya*, underneath and to the front. Tie the *sageo* through the *hakama* ties (*himo*). The tie is either a single loop pushed up between the ties, or a double loop (which is one loop inside another).

Exercise | Warm-up

Warm-up exercises include the use of the sword and general body movements similar to other arts. Primarily the emphasis is on the sword warm-up moves, to work the relevant parts of the body prior to technical practice, and using either a *bokken* (wooden replica) or *shinken* (live blade), depending upon level of qualification.

WARM-UP 1 – *This vertical cutting technique is known as* kirioroshi.

❶ △ Draw your sword into the centre ready position (*chudan kamae*). Keep an upright posture with shoulders relaxed, back straight and the heel of your rear foot slightly raised. Your right hand is near the sword's guard (*tsuba*) and your left hand is towards the end of the handle (*kashira*). Make sure the V shape of your hand is uppermost on the *kashira*, with your thumb and forefinger on either side.

❷ △ Ensuring your grip is secure yet relaxed, raise the sword above your head (*jodan kamae*), ensuring that the tip of the blade remains horizontal. When cutting, avoid a hard grip, since this burns up unnecessary energy, which thus restricts your technique.

❸ △ Step forwards as you start to extend your arms fully in a "reaching" action, and commence a large, circular cut. The technique finishes with the sword at your waistline. Make sure you are looking straight ahead, maintaining the same body posture.

❹ △ Once the sword has completed its cutting action, the tip of the blade (*kissaki*) should be in line with the *habaki* – the metal fixture about 1 in (2.5 cm) long seated on the blade next to the *tsuba* between the handle (*tsuka*) and sword.

WARM-UP 2 – *The horizontal cutting technique is called* nukitsuke.

❶ ◁ With the sword in your right hand, held across your body, the blade should be level with your upper left arm with the tip pointing backwards. Using a large, circular action across your body, swing the sword back towards your right shoulder. The tip of the blade should be approximately in line with your right nipple. *Note: this cut is usually performed against an opponent in a sitting position, aiming for the eyes. When performed against a standing opponent, the target area is either the chest or abdomen.*

❷ ▷ Cut in a circular action. Your left hand plays an important part in all sword techniques, as it assists with the drawing of the blade. Make sure the left hand pulls the *saya* round the small of the back in a horizontal action. This action is simultaneous with the drawing action. The tip of the blade is level with the right side of the chest, at about nipple height.

Technique | First level

The following is a selection of techniques taken from particular styles known as *muso jiki-den ryu*, *eishin ryu*, and *oku-iai*. Once familiar and competent with *seitei gata iaido*, practitioners move on to practise the other *kata* within their chosen style. The intention is to develop not only the skill of drawing and cutting, but also the strategy behind the form.

TSUKI KAGE

△ *Tsuki kage* is a *kata* designed to enable the practitioner to draw and cut from a side attack. The aim is to draw the sword from a low posture, moving underneath the opponent's arms as the opponent attempts a cut to the head. This is an upward cut to both wrists. A variation is to cut just the right or left wrist.

YAE GAKI

△ The first technique is taken out of a form (*kata*) called *yae gaki*. You perform this technique towards the end of the *kata*, when your opponent is on the floor and is making a final cutting action at the lower part of your leg. To prevent the cut, use the side of your sword (*shinogi*) in a blocking technique, before preparing to make the final cut.

TSUKE KOMI

△ This move is taken from the last part of the *kata* known as *tsuke komi*. It demonstrates the "blood wipe" action following the final cut, which is one way of cleaning the blade before sheathing (*noto*).

OROSHI

△ *Oroshi* is a cut made to the side of your opponent's neck.

SEITEI GATA IAIDO

Today, many practitioners of iaido practise *seitei gata iaido*. This comprises a set of basic forms (*katas*) used in most styles of iaido to encourage uniformity in practice, so that people can be graded to a common standard. This, however, does not exclude the classical styles that are a part of iaido. Iaido is about strategy, and many of the forms demonstrate the importance of interpretation, timing, positioning, skill, vision and other qualities needed to survive in the day of the *samurai*. Today, these qualities are essential to the development of good character.

FORMS (*KATA*)
Performed from a sitting *(seiza)* **position**

Number	Name	Meaning
Ippon me (1)	*Mae*	Front
Nihon me (2)	*Ushiro*	Rear
Sanbon me (3)	*Uke nagashi*	Catch and slide off
Yonhon me (4)	*Tsuka ate*	Strike with the *tsuka* (handle)

Performed from a standing posture

Gohon me (5)	*Kesa giri*	Cross cut
Roppon me (6)	*Morote tsuki*	Thrust with both hands
Nanahon me (7)	*Sanpo giri*	Cut in three directions
Hachihon me (8)	*Gan men ate*	Strike to centre of face
Kyubon me (9)	*Soe te tsuki*	Thrust with supporting hand
Juppon me (10)	*Shiho giri*	Four-direction cut

Technique | Advanced level

The following shows a selection of techniques taken from a *kata* performed in the *muso jikiden eishin ryu* style. The first two pictures demonstrate one of the cuts in *iwanami*, which means "waterfall", followed by a sequence of moves taken from *taki-otoshi* against a rear attack.

TATE HIZA – Start position.

△ This position is called *tate hiza*, meaning "standing knee". The *samurai* used to sit in this fashion, since when they were wearing armour they could not easily sit in the normal sitting (*seiza*) position. The above position involves sitting with your left leg tucked under your body and your right leg slightly forwards and bent at the knee. This is a difficult posture for many Westerners to adopt, especially those with long legs. The Japanese are usually smaller in stature and are more easily able to sit in this position.

Finishing kneeling position.

△ This is the finishing posture at the end of some of the techniques performed in *eishin ryu* and *oku den*. After the cut, place the sword back in the scabbard (*saya*) – this is known as the *noto* movement. Next, bring your right foot back towards the left, maintaining a stable posture.

IWANAMI

❶△ This is part of the *iwanami kata* where you have turned and drawn your sword to your right side, taking hold of the blade with your left hand.

❷△ Following the preparation to strike, you thrust the sword upwards and forwards into the stomach region. There are several other moves before this *kata* is complete.

❸△ Using the *bokken*, we can practise the striking part of this technique to develop the take down which forms part of this *kata*.

❹△ This demonstrates the *hiki taoshi* movement, in which the opponent is pushed down on to the floor by placing the blade of your sword (*bokken*) on their right shoulder. This requires effective hip and body movement to be successful.

Technique | *Okuden*

Okuiai (or *okuden*) is one of the advanced levels offering a selection of standing and sitting forms using a variety of strategies to defeat the opponent. For example, a *kata* called *shinobu* (stealth – tapping the ground), in a scenario of darkness, encourages the opponent to make the first cut so that you know their position and can defend yourself.

TAKI OTOSHI

❶ △ This is the first part of *taki otoshi*, where the opponent tries to grip the scabbard of your sword. As you feel the grip, the intention is to go with the grab in a sequence of moves, to eventually disengage the opponent.

❷ △ Pushing the sword in a downwards motion weakens the opponent's grip of the sheath (*saya*).

❸ △ Keep the momentum going in an upwards direction to fully disengage the opponent's grip.

SODOME

△ Applying a stalking strategy, the intention is to cut three hidden opponents to the side of the neck, as you move forwards.

RYOZUME – *Restrictive movement against obstacle or wall.*

△ In view of the restriction, the sword is drawn very tightly in a forwards motion. This is followed by a lunge into the opponent.

Technique | *Uke nagashi*

The following pictures and captions are not fully instructional and are intended to show you an outline only of one of the *seitei gata iaido kata*. This *kata* is number three (*sanbon me*) and known as *uke nagashi* (catch and slide off). It demonstrates the strategy of defending against a single opponent to the side, from a kneeling position.

❶ ◁ Turn to your right side and kneel down. Take both hands off your sword and place them on your thighs.

❷ ▷ Look towards your imaginary opponent, who is about 6 ft (2m) away. Your opponent has drawn his sword, which he has positioned at the right side of his head (the technique of the sword being prepared at the right side of the head is known as *hasso kamae*). As he moves forwards, start to draw your sword and bring your left foot forwards, so that it is just in front of your right knee. Raise your sword upwards to deflect the opponent's downwards cut.

❸ △ As you stand, parry the cut by bringing your right foot to your left, as if standing "pigeon-toed". Your toes are not touching. This position ensures you are moving to the side of your opponent, to evade the cut and prepare the counter-attack.

❹ △ Pull your left foot back at about 18 degrees and cut down at a slight angle. Bring your left hand on to your sword as you turn in towards your opponent, and cut downwards at a slight diagonal angle, right to left (from your opponent's left shoulder to right hip).

❺ △ The cut will finish at a horizontal position and it is important to still maintain *metsuke* (direction of gaze – looking at your opponent and the wider environment) and *zanshin* (awareness), keeping alert in the event of any further danger.

6 ◁ Change your hand grip on the sword so that the blade is resting on your right knee.

△ This detail shows the correct hand grip once you have reversed the sword in preparation to returning it to its scabbard (*saya*).

7 ◁ Perform a reverse *noto* (sheathing the sword) by bringing the sword from the right knee, around the front of your body, so that it is positioned at the mouth of the scabbard (*saya*) – the open end of the *saya* is known as the *koiguchi*.

△ This is the hand and sword position at the beginning of the *noto*, before sheathing.

8 △ Lower your body, aiming to fully sheath the sword as your keft knee touches the ground. Keep looking (*metsuke*) to where your opponent has fallen, and be alert (*zanshin*) in case there are other opponents. Return to the standing position.

9 ▷ You can practise this particular *uke nagashi kata* with a real opponent, both of you armed with a wooden sword (*bokken*), but careful timing is needed to prevent injury. Working with a partner is useful, because it gives you a real feel for the blocking action, especially the correct angle of the sword, so that your opponent's blade slides off yours when it makes contact.

SHINTO RYU

Shinto ryu is a street defence strategy encompassing the "hard" (forceful self-defence) and "soft" (acceptance and deflection) elements of various martial arts styles. It has developed into a unique self-defence system suitable for all, irrespective of age, fitness or gender. Shinto ryu teaches practitioners skills they can adapt to any situation: hard techniques might be required in response to aggression or physical violence, yet shinto ryu's softer techniques might be more appropriate in an unsolicited or threatening situation.

SHINTO RYU

history *and* philosophy

The martial arts that are popular today originated and evolved, sometimes over many hundreds of years, from the concepts and ideas of visionary individuals whose belief systems and cultures moulded and shaped their skills and techniques. Today, new systems and styles continue to develop throughout the world.

Shinto ryu is one of the disciplines practised under the umbrella organization of the European Martial Arts Academy, and its name means "nature's way" or "spirit of nature" – *shinto* meaning "nature" or "shrine" and *ryu* meaning "the way". It is by understanding its name that we gain an insight into how the system works, by developing self-defence skills in a "natural way".

The Junior Defence Line specializes in developing the well-being of children and young people, and works within the European Martial Arts Academy. It offers a basic street defence system for children and young people, to help them feel more confident and capable of protecting themselves in the street and at school. Bullying is a major problem within many societies and most bullies are usually cowards. Yet their victims can be traumatized and scarred for life. The principles of shinto ryu spill into this very important area of developing good attitude, discipline and respect.

Children develop confidence by learning how to defend themselves against an aggressive attack. Physical defence is encouraged as a last resort.

Underlying principles

The philosophy of this discipline never manifests itself in seeking harm. Instead, it strives to equip practitioners with techniques that allow them to walk away from difficult situations. Defusing techniques are of paramount importance, but we need confidence to use these skills effectively.

Emphasis is placed on restraining techniques. Street clothing and foot wear are encouraged in some training sessions, to give a feeling of reality.

Having knowledge of the physical skills we can put into practice at times of threat and danger can increase our confidence to handle a particular situation. Our body language gives away a great deal about us – research has identified that many victims of street crimes looked like victims before any aggression occurred, and it is possible to minimize risk by looking more confident. We only have to look at the posture used in many of the martial arts. The upright relaxed posture, with shoulders back and looking forwards, projects a perception of awareness, confidence and strength. As Musashi Miyamoto, one of Japan's most famous swordsmen (1584–1645), once said: "Perception is strong and sight is weak!"

Part of shinto ryu is learning once more to trust our intuition, an attribute that we have become complacent about in today's technological and materialistic society. How many times have you felt uncomfortable about a person you have been introduced to, and sometime later this person does something to harm you in some way? Recalling your initial feelings, you say to yourself, "I knew I could not trust that person", and yet you still allowed that situation to develop, not having the confidence to listen to your gift of intuition.

Shinto ryu in practice

Shinto ryu is a modern discipline. Practical techniques are taught based on a "star" movement, which allows you to defend yourself from any conceivable angle – whether standing or seated. Reality is the key to this system of self-defence. Practitioners are taught how to respond to different real-world situations, such as being threatened on public transport, for example, in cars, at work and many other environments. Shinto ryu also teaches you how to improvize with objects you are likely to have at hand, such as using a chair or small table as a barrier, as part of a self-defence strategy.

The use of a *shinai* (bamboo stick) has also been incorporated, but not in the same way as in the art of kendo. It is used to replicate a potential weapon such as a piece of wood, iron bar or pole that may be at hand, so that the practitioner can learn to strike and defend effectively.

BENEFITS OF SHINTO RYU

The benefits derived from learning shinto ryu affect many aspects of your everyday life. These include:

- Speed and agility
- Fitness and stamina
- Awareness and intuition
- Self-confidence
- Self-control and well-being
- Precision and timing
- Respect and self-discipline
- Comradeship
- Inner peace and calm
- Stress reduction
- Character development

Exercise | Warm-up

The following is a sample of some of the exercises performed in shinto ryu prior to training. Certain advanced exercises are not taught to children as they may cause harm. The following is performed by an experienced young man. Please remember it is important to build up exercises slowly for maximum benefit.

WARM-UP 1 – *Leg stretch to strengthen inner thighs.*

△ From a standing position, bend your front (left) leg at an angle of about 90 degrees, while keeping your rear (right) leg straight. Push forwards to stretch your inner thigh. Repeat this exercise with your right leg forwards. Hold the tension for 5–10 seconds, change to your left leg and repeat the exercise 3–4 times.

WARM-UP 2 – *The splits are excellent for stretching your inner thighs.*

❶ △ With legs astride, gently lower your body as far as you can. It may take some months before you can fully reach the floor. Only go as wide as you comfortably can and practice on a regular basis to improve your suppleness in this exercise.

❷ △ The ultimate aim of this exercise is to be able to lower your head down to touch the floor. This increases the pressure on the inner thighs. Lean forwards, pushing your head down as far as you comfortably can.

WARM-UP 3 – *Press-ups assist in developing the top part of the body.*

△ With the palm of your hands down, feet together and body straight, gently lower your body to the floor. Do not touch the floor but keep your body elevated about 1–2 inches (2.5-5 cm). Push back up to the starting position and repeat. Breathe out as you lower your body, and in as you push back up. *Caution: only perform this exercise 2–3 times and build up gradually. Children under 11 should not perform this exercise, except for a modified version, on knees, and under qualified supervision.*

WARM-UP 4 – *Back and leg stretch for suppleness.*

△ Lower your body so that you can place your right leg to the side and your left knee facing forward at a 90 degree angle. Take hold of your right ankle with your right hand and lower your head towards your right knee. Keep your leg straight for maximum stretch. Do not be concerned if you cannot touch your knee in the early stages, as this will come with practice. Only lower yourself to a position that feels comfortable, pushing a little further each time. Change to the left leg and repeat the exercise 3 times each side.

Technique | Children's self-defence

Shinto ryu seeks to develop all our senses, capabilities and skills to the maximum, and arm us to deal with any difficult situation wisely and safely. While it may be perceived that only the fit and young can practise a martial art, rudimentary skills can be applied to a defence situation by all ages, gender and abilities.

DEFENCE 1 – *Children can apply the power of the circle very effectively to disengage an attack.*

❶ ◁ The attacker makes a double-handed grab, pulling you off the ground.

❷ △ Take hold of the aggressor's thumbs with both hands.

❸ △ Using an outwards circular motion, pull the aggressor's thumbs down. This will cause pain and encourage the aggressor to let go and allow you to escape.

DEFENCE 2 – *This demonstrates how children can use their strengths against an aggressor's weaknesses.*

❶ △ The aggressor moves in with a single-handed grab to your body.

❷ ▷ Step back to create distance and bring the knife edge of your right hand up in a semi-circular motion to deflect the grab. Slide your hand down towards the aggressor's hand and take hold of his wrist or, if you have a small hand, as much of his hand as you can take hold of. It is important to keep this as a continuous action, since it is the momentum and the body movement which enhance the success of the technique.

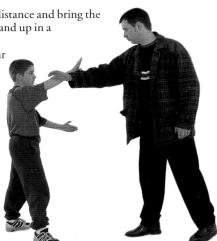

△ Even though you may have a small hand, taking hold of the aggressor's little fingers and using the power of the circle, can assist in breaking a grip.

❸ ▷ As you continue the circular action with your right hand, bring your left hand up under the aggressor's right elbow to assist the action. If you find this difficult, as the aggressor is moved downwards, bring your forearm across his elbow and your body forward, keeping the momentum and control towards the floor. From this position either throw away, as you have prevented the grab, or continue to restrain, depending on the situation.

△ As the circular action continues, the aggressor's palm should turn upwards so that pressure can then be applied to the elbow.

❹ △ Keep applying pressure by rotating the hold, which, in turn, will assist in pushing the aggressor to the floor. Keep your body weight over the elbow joint to secure the pressure. Call for assistance or leave the area.

DEFENCE 3 – *Disengaging safely against a hair grab.*

1 △ An aggressor moves in and grabs your hair with the intention of pulling you back and off balance.

2 △ Bring both your hands up above your head. Remain upright or slightly lower your position, depending upon the size of the aggressor. Either way, it is important not to lean back.

3 △ Place both hands on top of your head and lock your fingers together. Push down firmly to apply a locking technique on the aggressor's hand. This will minimize the pain of having your hair pulled and start the disengagement. If you have small hands, attempt to find the most comfortable grip for you, ensuring your fingers are securely locked together, and press down. As you turn, you may find your hands starting to grip the wrist. This is acceptable if it assists in maintaining control by turning the aggressor's arm.

4 △ Continue to turn your body in towards the aggressor, maintaining a firm grip.

5 △ As you almost complete your turn you will feel his grip start to loosen. Be aware of his other arm and legs at all times, in the event he may try to strike. *Note: the faster you apply this turn, the easier it is to encourage him to let go, through the pain inflicted on his joints, tendons and muscles.*

6 △ At the end of the turn, the aggressor should have released your hair. To maintain control bring your thumbs around on to the top of the aggressor's hand. Apply pressure with the thumbs in a forwards and downwards motion. Then, either push the aggressor away or apply a "hard" technique, such as a kick to the solar plexus or face (depending upon the seriousness of the attack). If you are in an isolated area you may need to apply a hard technique to incapacitate the aggressor for a long period of time. A unique aspect of shinto ryu is the fact that, whilst training occurs within the traditional environment, emphasis is also placed on training in various surroundings e.g. in parks, the street, home or work. In other words, it is applicable in every-day situations and in everyday clothes.

Technique | Women's self-defence

Women's self-defence features strongly in shinto ryu, with its modern outlook. Handling more than one aggressor at the same time may be viewed as an impossible task, but it is important to apply a strategy that utilizes your strength to maximum effect against an aggressor's weaknesses, so that you can safely escape from a difficult situation.

CAUTION

As an initial strategy, it is always best to avoid conflict by applying such skills as verbally de-fusing the situation, body language and similar strategies. If this does not work, only then, as a last resort, apply physical self-defence, using "reasonable force" to protect yourself (or others). Even if you successfully defend yourself, an aggressor may have the right to sue you. The law varies from country to country and you may be called on to prove that reasonable force only was used. It is, therefore, preferable to use restraining techniques, depending upon the seriousness of the situation.

1 △ One of the aggressors grabs your wrist with his right hand. If you have an item such as an umbrella, make use of this in your defence. Apply a circular action with your wrist (the same technique used with or without an umbrella) to disengage the grab.

2 △ If you do have an umbrella to aid your defence, twist to position it over the aggressor's wrist. Bring your left hand underneath and take hold of the umbrella to lock the aggressor's wrist. Push down to apply pressure and take the aggressor to the floor.

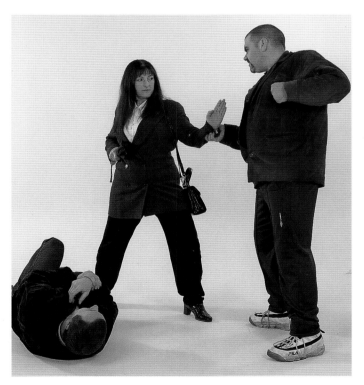

3 △ Usually, if you successfully disengage the first aggressor, other aggressors can be dissuaded from continuing with the assault. Where this is not the case, apply the power of the circle to disengage the grab and strike to a weak point, such as the face or throat. *Caution: this is the last-resort application, when all else has failed, and when you believe your life is in imminent danger. When practising with a partner, focus (aim) your technique – do not make contact.*

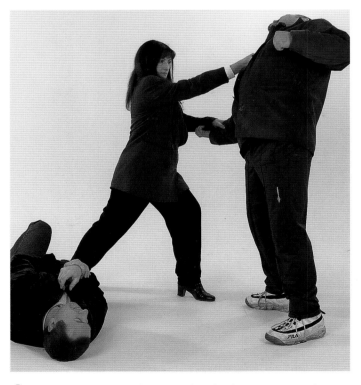

4 △ Strike to the vulnerable area, such as the throat. *Caution: this is an extremely dangerous area to strike and should only be used as a last resort in a serious situation.*

Technique | Disengagement

Being grabbed about your body, wrist, arm, shoulder or clothing is another type of assault. Ideally, always try to talk your way out of the situation and keep a safe distance between you and the aggressor. However, if an aggressor moves in to grab you, it is important to try to disengage the grip before you are physically struck.

BODY GRAB – *Defence against a body grab.*

❶ ◁ An aggressor makes a grab with his right hand to your left lapel.

❷ ◁ Place your left hand completely over the aggressor's right hand, aiming to lock his thumb and fingers. Keep close to your chest for maximum control and start to pull outwards to cause the aggressor to release his grip. At the same time, depending upon the circumstances, strike to the nose. This will cause the eyes to water which, in turn, will obscure the aggressor's vision and give you a chance to escape.

❸ ◁ Following the strike, bring your right hand under the aggressor's right arm and take hold of his right hand. You are now preparing to throw the aggressor to the floor.

△ Close-up of both hands gripping the aggressor's right hand in preparation to throw.

❹ △ Continue the momentum of the arm movement forward, while at the same time stepping through. You need to ensure you are very close to the aggressor to break his posture and balance. Remember that these techniques are successful only when applied with correct timing, skill and body movement.

REAR DEFENCE – *Defence against a grab from the rear.*

1 △ As the aggressor grabs you with his right arm around your throat from the rear, immediately try to drop your chin downwards, to alleviate any pressure against your throat. At the same time, turn your body inwards towards the aggressor and aim to take hold of thumb and fingers.

2 △ Pull the aggressor's arm forwards, locking his elbow on top of your right shoulder. Ensure that you push the aggressor's palm outwards, with his fingers pointing downwards for maximum effect. Keep your body upright to maintain pressure on his elbow joint.

3 △ Using a circular motion, bring the aggressor's arm around your right side, preparing to throw him. Although a smaller child may find this throw awkward to execute, it should present little difficulty for a teenager or adult.

4 ▷ The aggressor will be winded, or at least disorientated, as he lands on the floor. This will incapacitate him, allowing you time to escape. If there is any possibility that the attacker could still be a threat, strike with a leg technique of your choice.
Note: remember the law and the use of "reasonable force". It is always best to incapacitate the aggressor with minimum force and get away to safety. However, depending upon the circumstances, you may have no alternative but to follow through with a further technique, to ensure you have enough time to escape.

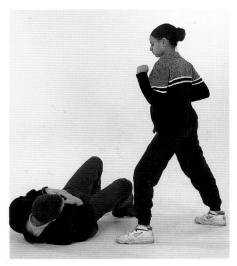

5 △ Continue to maintain an assertive attitude because, in spite of being floored, the aggressor could try to retaliate (or there may be other assailants close by). You may have been successful in your defensive manoeuvre, but don't be overconfident. Keep alert until you are safely out of the situation.

Technique | Knife defence

While a knife attack is unlikely, being prepared builds self-confidence. Shinto ryu encourages students to practise defence moves against weapons to ensure that people have the ability to defend and disarm should the need arise. However, the fundamental principle of defence should always be to verbally defuse the situation, if possible.

CAUTION

When training with a partner, use a plastic knife unless you are very experienced. If you use a real knife (only if under professional supervision), control the technique so that the knife does not fall indiscriminately. When practising, it is very important to respect any weapon and to be aware of the potential dangers.

DEFENCE 1 – *Demonstrating how to counter a knife face slash.*

❶△ A slashing knife attack is very frightening, but as the aggressor comes in, duck down to avoid the knife.

❷△ As the knife swings back round, bring your body up and block the aggressor's right arm with the edge of your right hand or fore-arm. Ensure you turn your body away from the knife attack as you block. Remember it is not the knife that is dangerous but the person using it!

❺ ▽ Keep the momentum going and take the aggressor to the floor. Ideally, pick up the knife, to prevent any further assault, before seeking assistance.

❸△ Twist completely around inwards, towards the aggressor, leading with your left foot. Spin your body clockwise so that you are facing the same way as the aggressor. Keep the knife away from you by bringing your left arm over the attacker's right arm, ideally aiming for just above the elbow joint, and take hold of your own right wrist. Apply pressure by locking your arms. Keep your body close to the side of the aggressor to maintain maximum control.

❹△ Pivot on both feet, turning in an anti-clockwise (counterclockwise) direction to face the aggressor. At the same time, apply a circular action to the aggressor's wrist, bending his elbow so that the knife ends up behind the aggressor. This continuous, flowing movement will cause pain, and should encourage the aggressor to drop the knife.

DEFENCE 2 – *Demonstrating how to defend against a knife body lunge.*

1 ◁ An aggressor moves in with a knife attack to the stomach. Side step the attack and block with your left arm, taking hold of the left wrist to stop the knife attack. This technique is one of many knife defences used in shinto ryu.

2 ▷ Place your left arm under the aggressor's elbow joint, and take hold of his right wrist with your right hand, to apply an elbow lock to release the knife.

3 ◁ If the aggressor has not already dropped the knife, this is the time to apply further pressure to release the weapon. Pin the aggressor's arm against your chest to apply pressure against the elbow joint, keeping the knife away from your body. Simultaneously move in and strike the hinge of his mandible (jaw bone close to the lower ear) with your left elbow. Remember, if the aggressor came in with a left-hand knife attack, you would apply the above from the opposite side.

index

A
armour, kendo, 90–1, 95
axe kick, tae kwondo, 64

B
back heel kick, tae kwondo, 65
back-hook kick, tae kwondo, 67
back kick, tae kwondo, 66
blocking forms:
  kick boxing, 52
  mok-gar, 34–6
bong sau (wing arm), 12
breaking techniques, tae
  kwondo, 67
butterfly knives, 14, 25, 39

C
centre-line theory, wing
  chun, 12–13
chi sau ("sticky hands"), 13, 19
children:
  shinto ryu, 121–2
  tae kwondo, 65
  wing chun, 20
chudan tsuki, kendo, 98
close punching, kick boxing, 51
clothing:
  iaido, 106
  kendo, 90–1
  kick boxing, 44
  mok-gar, 30
  tae kwondo, 58
  tai chi chuan, 74
  wing chun, 14
contact sparring, kick boxing, 50
crescent kick, tae kwondo, 67

D
disengagement, shinto
  ryu, 124–5
do, kendo, 98
downward kick, tae kwondo, 64
drilling stance, mok-gar, 37

E
equipment:
  iaido, 106–7
  kendo, 90–1
  kick boxing, 44
  mok-gar, 30
  tae kwondo, 58
  tai chi chuan, 74
  wing chun, 14

F
fighting stance, kick
  boxing, 45
front kick, tae kwondo, 65

G
grades:

kick boxing, 44
mok-gar, 30
tae kwondo, 58

H
hook, tai chi chuan, 78

I
iwanami, iaido, 112

J
jigeiko, kendo, 99
jumping side kick, tae
  kwondo, 64
jumping turning kick, tae
  kwondo, 66

K
katata (thrust), kendo, 99
kau sau (circling hand), wing
  chun, 18
kicks, tae kwondo, 64–7
knife defence, 124–5
knives, butterfly, 14, 25, 39
kote, kendo, 98

L
leg striking, tae kwondo, 64–5
locking and striking, tai chi
  chuan, 80
lok sau, 22–3

M
meditation, kendo, 92
men uchi, kendo, 99
mook yan jong (wooden dummy
  practice), 24

O
okuiai (okuden), iaido, 113
oroshi, iaido, 111

P
pegs, mok-gar, 39
posture, kendo, 96
punching, kick boxing, 51
pushing hands, tai chi chuan, 82

R
rear defence, tai chi chuan, 81
ryozume, iaido, 113

S
safety:
  iaido, 107
  kendo, 91, 92
  kick boxing, 50, 51
  tae kwondo, 63
seitei gata iaido, 111
shiai (competition), kendo, 96
shinai, kendo, 94, 96

shinken, iaido, 107
side kicks:
  tae kwondo, 65, 66, 67
siu so gee, mok-gar, 39
6½ point pole, 25
sodome, iaido, 113
stance:
  kendo, 96
  kick boxing, 45
"sticky hands", wing chun, 13, 19
striking techniques:
  kendo, 97
  tai chi chuan, 79–80
suburi, kendo, 94
swords:
  iaido, 107
  tai chi chuan, 74, 83

T
taan sau, 21
taki otoshi, iaido, 113
tate hiza, iaido, 112
tee chec, mok-gar, 39
three-section staff, mok-gar, 39
toi sau (pushing hands), 82
tsuba zeriai, kendo, 99
tsuke komi, iaido, 111
tsuki kage, iaido, 111
turning kick, tae
  kwondo, 64, 65, 67
twisting kick, tae kwondo, 64

U
uke nagashi, iaido, 114–15

W
weapons:
  iaido, 107
  kendo, 90–1
  mok-gar, 39
  tai chi chuan, 83
  wing chun, 14, 25
women:
  shinto ryu, 123
  tae kwondo, 63, 66
wooden dummies, wing
  chun, 14, 24

Y
yae gaki, iaido, 111

ACKNOWLEDGEMENTS

Clive Preece and his team, Derek Creedon, Derek Raybold, Elaine Adani and Kevin McClennahon, Eugene Codrington and his team, Father Seamus Mulholland and Juliette, Graham Kenning, Hiroshi Sugawara, James Sinclair and his team, Kerstie Hodrien, Kerry Elkins, Kevin Pell and Miguel Camacho, Mark Wolski , Neil Adams and his team, Paul Boyer and Chris Goodburn, Peter Brady and Cath Davies, Ron Sergiew and his team, Roy Preece and family, Robert Poyton and his team, Trevor Jones, the British Kendo Association, Lingus Dignam, and Mark Peters of Kai Ming Martial Arts Association for kindly making his *dojo* available in the Tai Chi section. David Mills of CIMAC . Haruna Matsuo Sensei, Ishido Shizufumi Sensei, Oshita Masakazu Sensei, Fujii Okimitsu Sensei, Fukura Sensei, Ide Sensei, Chiba Sensei, Kanetsuka Sensei, Hirori Sensei, Eddie Daniels, A Hunt and T Foster.

FOR GENERAL INFORMATION:
contact Goodman Multimedia on (+44) 0121 784 8268 or email: goodmanmultimedia@eclipse. co.uk
MODEL ACKNOWLEDGEMENTS:
tae kwondo: Fiona Newcomb, Terry Read, Stuart Penn, Carole Gameson, Lorraine Oliver, Dale Newcomb *wing chun:* Sifu Mark Phillips, Jocob Jaywant, Nathan Jaywant, Joshua Jaywant, William Jaywant, Avril Kinsley, Deborah Smith *mok-gar kuen:* Chris Goodburn *kick boxing:* Rachael Barton, Kevin McClennahon *tai chi chuan:* Steve Blatchet, Kathy Chi, Robert Poynton *shinto ryu:* Derek Creedon, Ava Preece, Sophie Preece, Veera Kaur, Jevanpal Singh Choudhary, Mark Fisher, Paul Yeomans, Neil Smith. (Jagman Singh and Amar Kaur Choudhary, Harpaal and Harbinder Kaur).